Introduction

• • • • • •

> "I, *(Name)*, Take you, *(Name)*,
> To be my *(wife/husband)*;
> **To have and to hold,** from this day forward,
> for better, for worse, for richer, for poorer,
> in sickness and in health, to love and to cherish,
> as long as we both shall live."

We take these vows when we marry, brimming with hope and commitment to maintaining a strong, stable marriage for as long as we both shall live. This beautiful sentiment expresses a heartfelt belief in the promise of a long and happy life together.

A poll by the Pew Research Center in November 2007 noted that most Americans regard marriage as the ideal state, with upwards of 80 percent marrying. A poll by *Parade Magazine* in September 2008 also reflects the importance placed on having someone "to have and to hold, to love and to cherish." In response to the question: "Why did you get married?" more than 80 percent answered, "For love."

We begin marriage with the firm conviction that our love will sustain us through the years and our marriage vows will protect us.

While most of us are very much in love and really *mean* the vows we take at the time we say them, we may not have considered just what's required to realize the dreams we have for our marriage.

In light of our much longer life spans today, making these promises is a huge commitment, so we need to be fully aware of what we're saying and what it means for the future.

While we may have every *intention* of keeping our promises, all too often we don't follow up with the actions and behaviors that are essential to making our intentions a reality.

This book will help you understand the need to translate your beliefs and intentions into actions. It will guide you in engaging in the behaviors that can allow you to reach your goal of having a strong, stable marriage.

It's critical to have some serious conversations about the meaning of the commitments you're making *before* you get married. It's tempting to wait until there are problems in the marriage to do this kind of talking about the tough stuff, but doing so may help achieve your goal of a lifetime with someone "to have and to hold."

It's not enough to talk only in general terms about your relationship and your hopes for it. As the saying goes, "The devil is in the details."

One of the details that couples tend to avoid discussing is the issue of maintaining monogamy throughout their marriage. In fact, the only time they may speak about it is if they use a version of the marriage vows that includes the phrase "forsaking all others, be faithful to him (or her)."

Preventing affairs, however, involves far more than just making an initial vow. It's not like getting a one-time inoculation—or even getting occasional booster shots. It's more like taking a pill every day for the rest of your life!

This book is written specifically for those couples who have *not* faced the issue of affairs—and want to prevent ever having

TO
Have AND
TO Hold

A Personal Handbook
for Building a Strong Marriage
and Preventing Affairs

[Previously published privately under the title *Preventing Affairs*]

PEGGY VAUGHAN

Newmarket Press
New York

[Originally published in 2008 under the title *Preventing Affairs* by Dialog Press]

This book may not be reproduced, in whole or in part, in any form, without written permission. Inquiries should be e-mailed to permissions@newmarket-press.com or write to Permissions Department, Newmarket Press, 18 East 48th Street, New York, NY 10017, FAX (212) 832-3629.

This book is published in the United States of America.

ISBN 978-1-55704-851-6 paperback

10 9 8 7 6 5 4 3 2 1

Library of Congress Cataloging-in-Publication Data
Vaughan, Peggy.
  [Preventing affairs]
  To have and to hold : a personal handbook for building a strong marriage and preventing affairs / Peggy Vaughan.
      p. cm.
  "Originally published in 2008 under the title Preventing Affairs by Dialog Press."
  Includes bibliographical references.
  ISBN 978-1-55704-851-6 (pbk. : alk. paper) 1. Marriage--United States. 2. Adultery--United States. I. Vaughan, Peggy. Preventing affairs. II. Title.
  HQ734.V383 2010
  646.7'8--dc22
                                2010013315

Quantity Purchases
Companies, professional groups, clubs, and other organizations may qualify for special terms when ordering quantities of this title. For information, e-mail sales@newmarketpress.com or write to Special Sales, Newmarket Press, 18 East 48th Street, New York, NY 10017; call (212) 832-3575 ext. 19 or 1-800-669-3903; fax (212) 832-3629.

Printed in Canada.

www.newmarketpress.com

For further information about Peggy's work, visit her website: www.DearPeggy.com

Also available from Newmarket Press:
The Monogamy Myth: A Personal Handbook for Recovering from Affairs
(978-1-55704-542-3, $14.95, paperback)

Contents

Personal Note from the Author

• • • • • •

In 1955, I married my childhood sweetheart. We were very much in love when we married and took our vows very seriously. We shared the same background, values and beliefs. So we entered marriage feeling confident that we would be able to nurture a strong, stable marriage.

I'm grateful that we have a close, loving relationship after all these years. And we do have the strong, stable marriage we had anticipated. However, it was a much greater struggle than I ever imagined it might be.

While we were quite successful in handling the typical problems that most couples face at one time or another, we were totally unprepared to deal with the one issue we never discussed: faithfulness.

We were like many couples who still enter marriage *assuming* their marriage will be monogamous. Our strong assumption was that couples who loved as much as we did were simply immune. So we were totally unprepared to discover that *anyone* could be vulnerable.

After my husband told me of his many affairs during a 7-year period (beginning after 11 years of marriage), we spent several years working through the ramifications, trying to understand what happened and whether and how we could recover and rebuild our marriage. Once we came to understand more about this whole issue, we used our experience to try to help others recover from the devastating impact of affairs.

Since 1980 when we wrote our first book and "went public" with our experience, I have devoted myself to helping others get more understanding and perspective as well. But through the years I came to see that it's critical to focus on *preventing* affairs in the first place—rather than only on picking up the pieces after an affair has taken place.

I became more serious about working on prevention after making a keynote speech on preventing affairs at the 1999 Smart Marriages Conference. During my presentation, I offered a professional assessment of the issue. Then at the conclusion of my talk, I unexpectedly broke into tears when I talked about wanting to protect my three granddaughters from growing up to be as vulnerable as past generations.

This personal concern provided additional motivation for working toward more understanding of what's involved in preventing affairs. I don't want future generations to continue this pattern of simply assuming monogamy—without the tools that are so critical to maintaining a long-term monogamous marriage.

I gradually began focusing more and more on prevention and began writing some articles about the issue. I searched for books on the topic and only found books like my own where prevention was a small part of the overall focus, but I found no book completely dedicated to prevention. So I felt the time had come to devote myself to researching and writing about preventing affairs—thus this book.

Author's Note: In keeping with accepted guidelines for nonsexist writing, extensive use of the pronoun *they* (especially the possessive form *their)* has been made when referring to a singular noun.

to face it. I've spent many years working to help couples recover from affairs, and I realize that one of the reasons they failed to prevent the affairs in the first place was that they had just *assumed* they would be monogamous. Since they never considered they might be vulnerable, they didn't actively work at preventing affairs—or even recognize it as an issue that needed to be discussed.

You CAN have a monogamous marriage, but not by just *assuming* you're immune. Having a long-term monogamous marriage requires knowing what's involved in preventing affairs— and acting on that knowledge on an ongoing basis as a couple.

Although you may have every intention of being monogamous and no idea of becoming involved in an extramarital affair, that doesn't make you (or your spouse) immune; in fact, no one is immune.

Here's the way I described this in *The Monogamy Myth:*

> *Monogamy is something most people say they believe in and want for themselves. Every survey ever done on this question shows a high percentage of people think monogamy is important to marriage and that affairs are wrong. But a belief in monogamy as an ideal doesn't prevent large numbers of people from having extramarital affairs.*
>
> *No one is immune from having affairs disrupt their lives or the lives of those they care about; they happen to all kinds of people, in all walks of life.*

When I first wrote those words in 1989, many people still held the false idea that "bad people have affairs and good people don't." But through the years, the public is coming to recognize that affairs also happen to good people in good marriages.

In fact, couples may be even more vulnerable to affairs when they hold the attitude that *"an affair could never happen in* our *marriage."* This has been the experience of many couples who felt good about their marriages (often being the envy of their friends), then discovered too late that *no* marriage is immune.

There's a great deal of denial and rationalization when it comes to focusing directly on the issue of affairs. So it's a "tough sell" to get couples to see that they can't just assume monogamy. Assuming monogamy is one of many false beliefs (myths) that make up "the monogamy myth." Unfortunately, this myth has not changed during the years since I first wrote about it.

For instance, I recently spoke to a woman who was newly married, and I asked her what kind of discussions she and her husband had about preventing affairs. She made a typical response: *"We didn't talk about it; we just* assume *we'll be monogamous!"*

One of the reasons so many people assume monogamy is because they think affairs happen only in a few marriages. People will say, *"Well, I don't know anyone who has had an affair."* My response is, *"Yes, you do know people who've had affairs; they just kept it secret and never told you about it."*

You're likely to learn of an affair only if it leads to divorce; however, the majority of couples stay together, often keeping the experience secret from friends and family. This secrecy creates a distorted view of the prevalence of affairs—because we tend to think that the few affairs that are disclosed are the only ones that happen.

The Prevalence of Affairs

The reason it's important for people to understand the prevalence of affairs is that without that understanding they have a false sense of security. And thinking they're not vulnerable makes it less likely they will put forth the necessary effort to prevent affairs.

Since so many people are desperate for evidence that affairs are not a big threat to them personally, they *want* to believe that affairs are not prevalent—and they gravitate toward any survey or study that provides some reassurance.

For instance, one prominent study a few years ago reported that only 25 percent of people have affairs. This is questionable due to the fact that statistics were higher than that way back in the 40s and 50s with the famous Kinsey studies. His samples included 5,000 men and showed that by age 40, 50 percent of the men had experienced extramarital sexual intercourse. And Kinsey's original samples of 6,000 women showed that by age 40, 26 percent of the women had experienced extramarital sexual intercourse. *Anyone who thinks there has been no increase in affairs during the past half-century is living in a dream world.*

Definition of an Affair

One of the reasons it's so difficult to establish an accurate measurement of the prevalence of affairs is that respondents to surveys often filter their responses through their own denial and rationalization about this issue. For instance, many people will report that they haven't had an affair based on their personal "definition" of an affair. They may consider a one-night stand or a brief fling while out of town or a massage that includes sexual aspects or paid sex of any kind *not* to be an affair. Likewise, many people consider an "online affair" or an "emotional affair" *not* to be an affair. And they bring these personal interpretations to their responses to the surveys that ask about having an affair.

Before going any further in discussing how to prevent affairs, it's important to establish just what constitutes an affair. Here's a working definition:

> Any outside relationship with a sexual or an emotional connection *that is kept secret from the spouse* is a threat to the marriage and can legitimately be defined as "an affair."

The Importance of Monogamy

There is evidence that monogamy is a very important issue for couples, as reflected in a 2007 report from the nonprofit Pew Research Center. The results of their interviews of 2,020 American adults showed that the top factor (seen as *most important to success in marriage*) was "faithfulness," chosen by 93 percent of those interviewed.

So if preventing affairs is viewed as the most important factor in marital success, it warrants making a major effort to be as informed and active as possible—despite the confusing statistics that make it difficult to know *precisely* how many affairs are happening.

However, regardless of the particular statistics as to how many men have affairs and how many women have affairs—those having affairs are not all married *to each other*. So the total number of *marriages* affected by affairs is necessarily larger than the numbers of either men or women having affairs.

In trying to get people to focus on the prevalence of affairs, I feel somewhat like a "voice in the wilderness" or the only one saying, *"The Emperor has no clothes."* But this awareness is essential if we are to help people prevent affairs—and to recover if it happens. It's only by recognizing the prevalence of affairs that couples will be adequately alerted to the need to take positive steps to achieve their hopes for a long-term monogamous marriage. I hope this book will be helpful in making this possible for more couples.

Survey on Preventing Affairs

In preparation for writing this book, I conducted a survey on my website. The respondents were self-selected, and this was not intended to be a scientific survey. I wanted to get a current indication of the most commonly held beliefs about prevention.

In order to help people be more effective in preventing affairs, I felt a need to know more about their current thinking.

I listed 16 items and asked people to choose the 5 that they thought were most likely to be effective in preventing affairs. (They could also add to the list by checking "other" and specifying what they would like to add to the list.)

Since attitudes about prevention are often determined by a number of very personal factors, I began the survey by asking people to identify themselves on three characteristics: gender, marital status, and personal experience in dealing with affairs. Below is a breakdown of the respondents:

Total Responses: 755

Gender:
575 women
180 men

Marital Status:
728 married
27 single

Personal Experience with Affairs:
552 yes
203 no

Results of the Survey

The results of this survey do not necessarily reflect the *actual* relative importance of the factors most effective in preventing affairs, only which are the most commonly held *beliefs* about which factors are most important. However, I did a careful count of the responses and provide a detailed list of the Rankings of all 16 items, with percentages choosing each item.

(See Appendix II for the full breakdown of percentages and rankings.)

Appendix II also includes breakdowns by subcategories, including:

- differences between women and men
- differences between those who are married and those who are single
- differences between those who have had personal experience in dealing with affairs and those who have not had personal experience.

The significance of the items is better understood by focusing on these breakdowns than by looking at the overall rankings. In fact, these breakdowns provide the most important information to be gained from the survey results.

Note that the data from the survey are included in the Appendices at the end of the book:

- Appendix I: A copy of the Questionnaire and overview of responses
- Appendix II: Rankings of all the responses to the Questionnaire

Part I

What WON'T Work
(Relying on Attitudes and Beliefs)

Each of the eight chapters in Part I focuses on an item in the Questionnaire that reflects an attitude or a belief that people hope will prevent affairs. These include:

Being in love with your partner
Having similar backgrounds and values
Having mutual trust
Having high moral principles and/or religious convictions
Taking the marriage vows seriously/intending to be faithful
Having children together and being a devoted mother/father
Concerns about consequences: hurting others, getting caught
Having no opportunity—no free time, never travel, etc.

As you read over the above list, do you find yourself agreeing that these are key factors in preventing affairs? If so, you're like a lot of people who rely on their "attitudes and beliefs" to keep them safe from temptation. Unfortunately, this way of thinking is relying on a set of myths that fall far short of the goal of long-term monogamy.

While each of these items is important in *establishing* a marriage that may be less vulnerable to affairs, it's only reflective of the starting point of the marriage. These myths are not sufficient to *maintain* a monogamous marriage over the long haul.

It *is* possible to prevent affairs over the course of a long-term marriage, but it involves far more than just relying on beliefs or intentions. Preventing affairs does not depend on a one-time decision or commitment (one of the key myths). It depends on pursuing the kinds of actions and behaviors that can sustain monogamy over the lifetime of the marriage.

The bottom line is that our initial "attitudes and beliefs" about preventing affairs need to be sustained and strengthened through ongoing "actions and behaviors"—which will be the focus of Part II. There you will learn about the specific strategies and techniques that *can* work!

Chapter 1

......

Being in love with your partner

Most people marry for love. There's a popular misconception that love is the be-all, end-all for a relationship, and this idea is perpetrated by TV, movies, magazines, and popular music. A good example is the Beatles' classic, *"All You Need Is Love."* In fact, they really grind this idea into the ground, repeating "All you need is love" over and over.

While love is an important aspect of marriage, it's not enough to sustain a couple through the years. Being in love with your partner definitely provides a good beginning to a relationship, but it's not a key factor in preventing affairs.

The Changing Nature of Love

Regardless of the strength of your love at the beginning of your marriage, love is not fixed in place, never to change. The fact is that love changes over time—which means it's smart to wait at least two years from the time you begin a relationship until you get married. This two-year wait is because this is about the time it takes for the newness to wear off.

This process has been clearly described by Helen Fisher in her book, *Why We Love: The Nature and Chemistry of Romantic Love.* The early stages of romantic love involve elevated levels

11

of dopamine and norepinephrine, leading to sweaty palms, a racing heart, and obsessive thinking about the loved one.

But it doesn't last beyond the first couple of years. At that time, the "cuddle chemicals" (elevated levels of oxytocin for women and elevated levels of vasopressin for men) take over, switching the "romantic" phase of love to the "attachment" phase.

Another way of understanding why romantic passion recedes with time is also explained by Helen Fisher. *"Evolution dictates that intense romantic passion eventually changes to a more peaceful connection. The enormous time and energy required for romantic passion works against building a safe social world in which to raise children."*

I first wrote about the changing nature of love in my book *Making Love Stay*. One of the biggest myths about love is the idea that "love never changes." Romantic love is just the first stage of love. Love changes; it never remains the same.

Enjoy new love for the fantastic experience that it is, but recognize that much of the intensity of the feeling is inherent in its newness and novelty. No, love is not magic. It can feel magical when things are going right. But love is actually the by-product of all the attitudes and behaviors each of you brings to the relationship.

Holding on to the idea that love exists in a vacuum only reinforces the false notion that the magical feeling of the first flush of new love is synonymous with love in its full, lasting richness (the kind that provides a firm place to stand in the world).

Love is not so different from a plant in that it too needs nourishment and ongoing attention in order to grow. Consciously doing loving things in a timely way is essential to making love stay. But you're busy, you're distracted by other things—and you still see the plant through the image in your mind's eye of its initial beauty when you bought it. Meanwhile, it's gradually losing its vitality—and if you wait too long to notice what's happening, it may be too late.

The Changing Nature of Sex

Just as love changes during the course of a long-term marriage, so does sex. In the beginning of a marriage, it usually feels like love and sex are completely bound together. Over time, when the sex may be less passionate, there can be a temptation to view this as a loss—not only of sex, but of love as well. This misunderstanding of the nature of love and sex can lead some people to say: *"I love him/her, but I'm not 'in love' anymore."*

While some affairs begin early in the marriage and are not triggered by a desire to recover the initial euphoria of new, passionate sex, over time this desire can lead to a greater vulnerability to an affair. Unfortunately, acting on this desire serves to reinforce the idea that great sex is defined by newness and excitement, which can lead to a lifetime of continuously seeking this kind of "high."

But getting a clearer understanding of the changing nature of sex can enable a couple to recognize the foolishness in trying to recapture the kind of unrealistic idealized romantic love/passionate sex they experienced in the beginning. Then they can more fully appreciate that they've simply transitioned into a more mature, accepting love—which can actually energize a couple sexually. Couples who come to really know each other and feel connected in a special way are prepared to move bravely forward into the deeper, richer nature of love and sex that's possible when they come to a fuller understanding of the possibilities.

Survey Results for "Being in love with your partner"

Ranked #11 out of the 16 items on the list

24.5 percent of total respondents chose this among their top 5 items

All percentages below reflect how many respondents chose this among their top 5 items.

Overall, men's and women's responses were not drastically different. (There were greater differences when we look at breakdowns based on criteria other than gender.)

23 percent of women

31 percent of men

Difference between marrieds and singles of both genders

There was a significant difference based on marital status. Singles ranked "love" #6, tied with "morals," while marrieds ranked it #10, tied with "similarities."

24 percent of all married respondents

37 percent of all single respondents

Those who are single hold more strongly to the idea that love can dictate the course of the relationship, while married people have already experienced the changes in the nature of their love. This experience gives them a clearer understanding of the fact that love won't protect them from affairs.

I was like many women who assume that *"If my husband loves me, he won't have an affair. And if he has an affair, it means he doesn't love me."* It was only after coming to understand the changing nature of love that I could believe he still loved me, despite having affairs.

Difference between married women and single women, both with experience

The biggest difference in the belief that "love" was a significant deterrent to affairs was between married women with personal experience and single women with personal experience.

21 percent of married women with personal experience

55 percent of single women with experience in an affair with a married man

This is an example of single women involved in affairs believing that one of the primary reasons for the affair is "love." They buy the old stereotype that a man having an affair must no longer love his wife. Also, women having affairs tend to believe that it's more about "love," while for the man it may be more about sex.

Difference between single women who have (and have not) had an affair

Single women viewed the importance of "love" quite differently based on whether or not they had had personal experience with affairs.

31 percent of single women who had *not* had an affair with a married man

55 percent of single women who had had an affair with a married man

This is another indication of the way single women who have been involved with married men still fall for the idea that the married man doesn't love his wife, and that he's having an affair with them because he's in love with them. They also believe the "in love" feelings in the affair are somehow special or meaningful or significant.

Comments about Results for "Love"

The initial feelings of being in love (that may happen in an affair) are quite different from the kind of love in a long-term

15

relationship. In fact, the difference is a little like comparing apples and oranges.

This difference is based on understanding that love changes as it goes through various stages. The "in love" feelings are just the first stage and are based on the flush of euphoric feelings that happen in the beginning of *any* new relationship—whether in an affair or as part of the initial dating relationship that led to the marriage in the first place.

For instance, it's likely that the love a man feels for his wife has shifted to the "attachment" stage while the love he feels for the other woman is still in the "romantic" stage. In fact, most affairs last less than two years—which directly corresponds to the point at which the feelings of romantic love begin to wane as the newness wears off.

It's not just the single woman in an affair with a married man who fails to understand this dynamic. Many people have come to think of the initial feelings of romantic love as the "real thing." While there may be no way to convince someone who holds this fantasy in their heads, it's important to recognize that this initial feeling does not define the nature of love.

What is "Love"?

I must admit that accurately defining "love" is problematic on the face of it. In the U.S. and many other countries, romantic love (feeling "in love") has become accepted as *the* definition of love. But as we are now coming to understand, this is just the first stage of love that doesn't last in this form. A more accurate definition of love is "love that lasts beyond the initial stage."

It's easy to kid yourself that you have a degree of intimacy with someone when you first meet, particularly if you get involved in sex right away. But this initial feeling of intimacy doesn't last, partly because it's a superficial sensation based on the newness of the relationship.

What happens in an affair is that people fall into "lust" during the first stage of romantic love and *feel* that this involves intimacy. But this is not the kind of true intimacy that comes only in the context of a love that develops over a period of time and becomes deeper and richer as you develop a full, satisfying relationship in all aspects.

Once you understand the changing nature of love, it's easy to see how the earlier "romantic love" feelings for your spouse (that have changed into an "attachment love") are not likely to serve as the kind of deterrent to affairs that many people hope or believe.

The Bottom Line about "Love"

"Being in love with your partner" creates an initial bond that can help sustain you through dealing with many of the difficulties you may face in a long-term marriage. However, its ability to do that depends upon recognizing (and embracing) the changing nature of love. Since the initial flush of romantic love doesn't last in that form, the feelings of love that began as a positive can become a negative if it leads to turning to someone outside the marriage for that "new love" feeling.

So love needs to be nurtured and deepened through the years if it's to contribute to preventing affairs. Otherwise, the desire to recapture the "in love" feelings that are typical of the first couple of years of romantic love can not only fail to prevent affairs, but can actually contribute to them.

Chapter 2

• • • • • •

Having similar backgrounds and values

Most people believe it's important to marry the "right" person. While it's smart to marry a person with values and qualities you admire and agree with, this is only the first step in a very long process of determining whether or not you are a good fit over the long haul.

For instance, the background of the man I married was almost identical to mine. Both of us were born and raised in Mississippi. We lived in a very small town where "everybody knew your name." We lived across the street from each other during pre-school years, began first grade together, and were in the same class for the next twelve years.

Not only did we have similar backgrounds, but our life experiences were similar as well, so we were able to start on the same page in our married life. This made for a smoother beginning to marriage than when two people come together with little in common in terms of background and values.

However, while beliefs, values, and priorities provide a good foundation, they may change over time—which is what happened to us. So it's essential that a couple maintain ongoing communication about the ways in which they are changing and demonstrate their commitment through the kind of *actions* that reinforce their beliefs.

Marrying Your "Soul Mate"

You may be tempted to believe that there is one special person meant just for you—that somewhere in the world is your soul mate, if only you can find them. So with the first flush of romantic love, many people may feel they've found their soul mate.

There is an old Gene Kelly song that says: *"You were meant for me, and I was meant for you."* Unfortunately, this reflects the thinking of many people, but the idea that any particular relationship was "meant to be" is just a romantic illusion, not rooted in reality.

At the beginning of a relationship, people present a side of themselves that's not representative of the whole person. The kind of intimacy that develops when people disclose themselves to each other in the early stages of a relationship is based on a fantasy image of the other person, not on a realistic perception of them. In fact, you don't really *know* them in any real sense, and the close feelings that often develop are due only to the newness of the relationship.

That's another reason it's wise to wait at least two years from the time you begin a relationship before you consider getting married. It takes time to really get to know another person to the extent required to successfully build a life together. While you may hear anecdotal stories of people who married after a brief courtship and stayed married for many years, the reason you hear these stories is specifically because they're unusual, the exception to the rule.

The idea of "finding your soul mate" makes it sound like love is some magical, mystical thing, removed from everyday reality. However, you can't *find* a soul mate; you can only work toward *becoming* soul mates as you get to know each other on a deeper, more trusting basis.

Frankly, it's quite rare for a couple to truly become soul mates, and it happens only after a great deal of commitment and experience in developing deep trust and true intimacy—which cannot be achieved quickly.

My personal experience reflects this pattern. James and I thought we were soul mates when we married. We felt sure we had a special love that would hold us together—no matter what. In fact, the strength of our initial romantic love was enough to sustain us for quite a while. But, like most couples, over the years the responsibilities of marriage and parenthood reduced the focus on the purely romantic part of our connection.

In fact, it wasn't until we'd been married for eighteen years that we finally began to really know each other—and to become soul mates. It was at that point that we faced a real crisis in our marriage: James's extramarital affairs, about which we have written extensively. In dealing with the affairs, we committed to a kind of rock-bottom honesty that laid the foundation for an unshakable trust and a deeper connection than we had thought possible.

Once we really got that, we've never wavered in our total commitment to honesty, to really knowing each other, to being connected in the world together. This kind of connection goes beyond being lovers; it goes beyond being married or being parents and grandparents or being friends or partners. It's a much more powerful connection that cannot be broken, no matter what.

Finally, holding on to the idea of finding a soul mate actually increases the vulnerability to having an affair. That's because once the "newness" is gone in a long-term marriage, the romantic feelings associated with affairs may cause people to again mistakenly think they've found their soul mate.

Realistically, the chance of finding a soul mate through an affair is even less likely than winning the lottery—and a lot more costly.

Survey Results for "Having similar backgrounds and values"

Ranked #10 out of the 16 items on the list

24.8 percent of total respondents chose this among their top 5 items

All percentages below reflect how many respondents chose this among their top 5 items.

The percentages were consistent between women and men.

25 percent of women

24 percent of men

Married men (with and without personal experience) made similar choices.

22 percent of married men with personal experience

26 percent of married men with no personal experience

However, married women's opinions were significantly affected by their personal experience. Those women with personal experience had learned firsthand that the similarities did not serve as a deterrent to affairs, while those without personal experience continued to believe that similar backgrounds and values would be an important factor.

21 percent of married women with personal experience

37 percent of married women with no personal experience

The most striking difference in the responses to this item was between those who were married and those who were single. Those who were still single (and still looking for "Mr. or Ms. Right") were likely to believe that similar backgrounds and values would be a significant factor. However, the experience of being married significantly diminished the expectations of "similarities" as a deterrent to affairs.

24 percent of all married respondents
44 percent of all single respondents

Comments about Results for "Similarities"

We see that those who are single and those who had no personal experience with affairs are far more likely to think that "similarities" have a more powerful influence than is the case with those who are married and those who have had personal experience.

In the abstract, there's a tendency to give more weight to choosing the right person, thinking this provides protection from affairs. But those like myself who married someone with a similar background and values still found our marriages vulnerable to affairs. Our similarities in the beginning did not protect us from affairs because we did not continue to have the same values as the marriage progressed.

Changes in Values and Priorities

Being similar in background and values only takes a couple so far—because people may change dramatically through the years due to exposure to different people and circumstances and different input from the world at large. So after a few years, the similar background and values lose their strength as a binding force. And this is the beginning of the really hard, ongoing work of keeping in touch with the changes taking place in the other person. A failure to do this means that at some point your spouse may seem so different from the person you married that you begin to wonder, "Who *is* this person?"

This is what happened to us. About ten years into our marriage, we had both changed dramatically, which significantly diminished the value of the initial similarities in background and values. At this point, each of us had developed new, very different, priorities.

Here's how my husband described these changes during the early years of our marriage: *"Our new lifestyle was well established. Peggy was a confirmed wife and mother. Those two roles formed her total identity. I was a professional psychologist, playing the university game to the hilt. Like most of my colleagues, I was a husband and father, but that was secondary to our work at the university. It was assumed that everyone had a family. The trick was not to let that interfere with your career. Without being aware of it, we had now settled into the mainstream of the American way of arranging family role responsibilities that sets the stage for one or both partners to lose interest in the marriage and gain interest in someone outside the marriage."*

So while similarities in background, experience and values prior to marriage can be a great asset to getting started on the right foot, it requires a sustained effort to maintain these similarities as the marriage and the individuals inevitably change over time.

Many people think that the way to avoid this kind of disconnect is to make an effort to share as many interests, activities, and experiences as possible. They fear that a failure to do so will cause them to "grow apart." This is a concern for many couples at some point in their marriage, and we shared some ideas about it in *Making Love Stay.*

Each of you will continue to change throughout your lives. You may be afraid of change—either yours or that of your partner. These changes need not be seen as threatening to the relationship. In fact, you will have a more interesting, exciting relationship if you are willing to share your goals and dreams and support whatever changes they entail. You may think you will grow apart if you change too much. As a consequence, you may try to avoid change (which is impossible) or try to control the change so that you grow in the same direction.

Despite how much you may have heard about "growing apart" as the cause of marital problems, it's an unfounded fear. The problems come not because of the changes themselves, but because of the failure to communicate about the ways in which you are changing. You and your partner don't need to avoid change or grow in the same direction in order to avoid growing apart. You simply need to stay in touch, to keep each other informed about your changes, and to support each other in the changes you choose to make. Don't worry about growing apart; that's unlikely if you clearly communicate on an ongoing basis.

The Bottom Line about "Similarities"

When two people come together with little in common in terms of their backgrounds, there can be many basic issues that create problems and tensions in trying to build a life together. So "having similar backgrounds and values" makes for a stronger beginning to married life.

However, people may change dramatically through the years due to exposure to different people and circumstances and different input from the world at large. So the initial similarities may have little impact on the degree to which a couple stay connected in a way that would help prevent affairs over the long haul.

So it's important to engage in honest sharing about the changes in values and priorities that both of you are sure to experience through the years. And the sharing needs to be on an ongoing basis if you are to develop the kind of strong bond that helps prevent affairs.

Chapter 3

• • • • • •

Having mutual trust

All too often the kind of trust we have in the early days of a relationship is based on *blind* trust. We may be blinded by our love and assume that trust should automatically follow when there's love. However, trust is not something you can just bestow; it's a natural by-product of trustworthy actions over time.

This doesn't mean we have to continually prove we're trustworthy. It just means that we're ultimately judged not by what we say, but by what we do. As the old saying goes, "Actions speak louder than words."

I personally know about this discrepancy between words and actions. During the period many years ago when I suspected my husband was having affairs, one of the reasons I ignored my doubts was because his words gave every indication that he was extremely trustworthy.

In fact, during that time he even wrote a poem that was published as a small book. And many years later we included it in *Beyond Affairs*, the book we wrote telling our personal story.

This poem illustrates just how confusing it can be when someone's actions don't match their words. For instance, he wrote this (and dedicated it to me) at the same time he was having affairs.

25

Please Trust Me

by James Vaughan

Please trust me, so that I can love you freely.
I need your trust to grow; without it I cannot be myself.
Your trust sets me free...gives me strength...
    helps me open myself to you...
Makes me rich...makes me feel ten feet tall...
    helps me accept myself...feels good.

I want to trust you. I will trust you if you care.
I need clear expressions of your caring for me.
I will trust you if you share...
I want to know who you are, what you feel, what you want,
    what you think...about life, about love, about me.

I will trust you if you dare...
We will change and grow together if we are not afraid
I want you to be part of my becoming
I want you to take the risk of hurting me
    in order to help me grow.

I want to be part of your becoming.
I will try to accept you as you are
    and help you become who you want to be.
Please let me.

I will never hurt you on purpose,
but I will run that risk in trying to help you grow.
I will make my trust known to you... with my eyes..,
with my touch.., with my presence.., with my words.

My trust for you will endure over time
    and become stronger each time we renew it.
It needs to be renewed so that it will reflect the changes in
    each of us.

If I should lose your trust,
    the weight of the loss would lie heavy on my shoulders.
Yet I would still be richer for having had it.
I will not do anything knowingly that would cause you to
    lose trust in me.

If I trust you deeply I will also love you deeply.
Trust is a delicate thing.
I may say or do something sometimes that causes you to
    doubt my trust.
Please share that doubt with me and check out my intentions.
I don't want to lose your trust.

There is no end to the depth of trust we can build.
Each time you show your trust in me
    my love for you grows deeper and I grow stronger.

Trusting you makes it possible for me to trust myself
    and others more.
When I trust my feelings and natural impulses and act
    on them, things usually turn out better.
That's hard to do sometimes.
Your trust helps me do it more often.

I need your trust now.
Time will never permit us to know each other completely.
But time need not stand in our way.
I have trusted deeply after four hours of sharing.

I have also found trust lacking after four years of working
together.

I don't need to know everything you have been
or everything you might become.
Let me know you now, and I will trust you now.
I know we need some time together, and yet our ability
to trust seems almost independent of time.

Trusting feels good...not trusting feels awful.
Experiencing deep trust with you makes me feel like...
time is standing still...
we are touching something precious...
we are reaching out for the highest part
of being human...
we are one with the universe.

I can feel your trust when you're not around...
it feels like warm sunshine.
When you touch me gently you affirm your trust in me.
I need your touch. I want it. It feels good.

There is power in trust—awesome power.
I can do much, much more when I know you trust me.
I will stretch myself to keep your trust.

I want to be all the things that I can be.
You can help me if you trust me.
I hope you will.

As I learn more about myself,
I will be able to trust you more.
Please help me learn.

The lesson from this example of a gap between words and actions is that it's important to pay attention to the actions, regardless of the words. And if doubts do arise, it's likely that they're being created by the fact that the actions don't match the words—and don't match the beliefs you may hold about your partner's trust.

Trust is not a simple aspect of a relationship that is either present or absent. There are many degrees or levels of trust; and at any moment in time, you and your partner may feel very different about the level of trust that exists between you.

Also, trust is not a once-and-for-all kind of thing. It's an ongoing dynamic between two people that may fluctuate over time based on what each person does (or doesn't do) that indicates the level of trust that's warranted.

You may feel anxious about whether you can trust each other without significantly restricting your mutual freedom. Realistically, neither of you can control the other by denying the other's freedom to pursue individual interests.

To keep your trust strong and growing, you need to constantly share your changing attitudes and beliefs. This is the only way to stay in touch with each other on an ongoing basis. So while you may begin with a high level of mutual trust, the level of trust changes throughout a relationship—based on actions that cause it to be either strengthened or diminished.

This increase or decrease in trust often depends on the degree of honesty that is maintained. In fact, honesty is one of the most powerful ways of building trust. And honesty includes a lot more than the words you say. It also includes being honest in your actions and your reactions, in the total way you relate.

(There's much more about this in Chapter 9 on "ongoing honesty.")

29

Trust-building depends not just on honesty about safe topics, but on being willing to risk disclosing your deepest thoughts and feelings, particularly your vulnerabilities. Trust depends on not putting on a mask or a false front about who you really are and what you really think and feel. In fact, if there's a temptation to withhold something about ourselves, it's especially important to share it. We can only fully trust when we are fully known.

Another factor in sustaining trust (and the intimacy that comes from that trust) is having a sense of fairness and equality in the relationship. If there's an imbalance of power and influence, the bond of trust will be weakened. And without that bond, you're unlikely to be able to maintain the kind of intimacy you want.

But when you're genuinely committed to fairness and equality and are willing to demonstrate that commitment in all areas of your lives together, your trust and intimacy will continue to grow.

Survey Results for "Having mutual trust"

Ranked #7 out of the 16 items on the list

34.8 percent of total respondents chose this among their top 5 items

All percentages below reflect how many respondents chose this among their top 5 items.

As with many of the items, the greatest differences in respondents' choices were between those with or without personal experience with affairs.

32 percent of all respondents with personal experience

41 percent of all respondents with no personal experience

The difference in opinion (based on whether or not there had been personal experience with affairs) was similar when the responses were broken down by gender. Both men and women with personal experience found "trust" to be less significant than men and women with *no* experience.

33 percent of married women with personal experience
45 percent of married women with no personal experience

29 percent of married men with personal experience
38 percent of married men with no personal experience

Comments about Results for "Trust"

Clearly, those with no personal experience held a stronger belief in the power of "trust" than did those who had already found through their experience that trust was not an effective deterrent. This is another instance of learning from experience that trust is not as strong a factor in preventing affairs as believed prior to having any experience.

In the beginning of your relationship, you may have felt a great deal of trust—which may or may not prove to be justified when you get to know the other person at a deeper level. The kind of trust in the early days of a relationship is very different from trust based on a deep knowing over time.

The Bottom Line about "Trust"

You don't get trust by seeking it directly; you only get it as a by-product of doing all the things mentioned in this chapter that lead to trust.

Trust needs to be renewed on an ongoing basis, which is best done by continually disclosing yourself. No matter how well you know each other in the beginning, everyone changes over time. In fact, each of us is a different person today than we were five years ago, and five years from now you will have changed in still more ways that you can't predict right now.

Trust is a dynamic characteristic of your relationship; it fluctuates constantly. The level of trust at any given time is a function of the attitudes, beliefs, and actions of both of you. So don't let blind trust cause you to ignore actions that don't confirm your trust. Remember that actions do speak louder than words.

Chapter 4

• • • • • •

Having high moral principles and/or strong religious convictions

As mentioned earlier, for many years the general thinking has been that "bad people have affairs and good people don't." This attitude is widespread, but it's wrong. In fact, affairs happen to good people in good marriages far more often than you might think. I often hear people say, *"I thought I had the best marriage of anyone I knew."* (My own husband said this, even as he was having affairs 40 years ago.)

Ironically, people in good marriages may believe they're immune. And, thinking they're safe from an affair, they may not actively work to try to prevent it from happening—thereby becoming *more* vulnerable.

Upon discovery of an affair, some of the most devastated spouses are those who believed their marriage was immune. For instance, those who are directly involved in religious work are often more shocked than others when they discover affairs have touched their marriage. Some of the most poignant comments were made by women in our Beyond Affairs Network (BAN) support groups who were married to clergymen.

Never in their wildest dreams would they have anticipated this could happen in their marriage, and they often felt

33

theirs must be the only such incidence. However, in one group there were six members who were married to clergymen who had affairs.

And those counselors who work specifically within a religious environment report similar incidences. For instance, Dave Carder, author of *Torn Asunder*, relates his experiences in intervening in several cases where clergymen abandoned their religious responsibilities to pursue an extramarital liaison.

There is a tendency to assume that if someone has an affair, then they are completely lacking in morals. However, there are many otherwise upstanding people who exhibit a great deal of integrity in all other areas of their lives who still fail when it comes to this particular temptation. While it's not reasonable to label people as good or bad based only on whether or not they succumb to an affair, it's obviously a huge deviation from the reasonable expectations we have of an otherwise moral person.

Unfortunately, I've discovered through the years that people who don't lie in any other important area of their lives may nevertheless be willing to lie about an affair. So while high moral principles and/or strong religious convictions may provide a good foundation for the likelihood of monogamy, these are *not* a guarantee. The fact is that all kinds of people from all walks of life have affairs, including people with "high moral principles and/or strong religious convictions."

Survey Results for "Having high moral principles and/or strong religious convictions"
Ranked #4 out of the 16 items on the list
41.9 percent of total respondents chose this among their top 5 items

All percentages below reflect how many respondents chose this among their top 5 items.

There was a clear difference between the responses of women and men.

38 percent of women

53 percent of men

Experience Differences

There was an even greater difference between those with personal experience and those with no experience.

34 percent of all respondents with personal experience

63 percent of all respondents with no experience

Among married women, there was a similar difference based on whether or not they had personal experience.

32 percent of married women with personal experience (ranked #8)

62 percent of married women with no experience (ranked #3)

Married men showed the most significant difference, based on whether or not they had personal experience. (In every comparison, it's clear that experience makes all the difference.)

39 percent of married men with personal experience (ranked #6)

73 percent of married men with no experience (ranked #1)

Comments about Results for "Morals"

While 41.9 percent of all respondents chose "morals" in their top 5, the percentages varied greatly when you looked at the breakdowns by gender, marital status and experience. (The overall responses to this and to most of the other items provide very little information/perspective compared with the breakdowns. This is where we can learn more about the realistic effectiveness of "morals" as a deterrent to affairs.)

In this case, the most valuable breakdown information is found in noting the difference that personal experience (or the lack thereof) makes in people's opinions about the importance of "morals" in preventing affairs. Those who had personal experience with affairs consistently viewed "morals" as less effective in preventing affairs than those without any experience. And the differences were consistent, regardless of gender.

The Bottom Line about "Morals"

While moral principles and religious convictions are certainly important aspects of the total person and may tell you something about their overall character, it's not wise to put a great deal of faith in these qualities to prevent affairs over the long run.

For instance, I vividly recall one woman's anguish as being particularly severe as she described finding out about her husband's affair. *"He was a pillar of society, big church man, never did anything wrong. I've been devastated."* Her shock was even greater because of having assumed he was not vulnerable.

Relying on the belief that morals and religious convictions will prevent an affair can bring a false sense of security, leaving people even more vulnerable to affairs because they don't pursue the kinds of actions that are essential to achieving life-long monogamy.

Chapter 5

• • • • • •

Taking the marriage vows
seriously/intending to be faithful
(Also recommitment: repeating/
renewing the marriage vows)

One of the reasons couples assume monogamy when they get
married is that they believe saying the words "forsaking all
others" in the vows constitutes some kind of guaranteed
protection from being vulnerable to affairs.

It's almost certain that most people do mean it when they take
those vows; they have every intention of remaining monogamous.
But it's not enough to make that initial commitment without
reinforcing it in other ways as the years go by. It's not reasonable
to lay so much of the burden of monogamy on the vows without
ongoing actions to reinforce that initial commitment.

Unfortunately, this magical belief that just taking the vows
guarantees monogamy for the duration of the marriage provides
a false sense of security. Even if a person has every intention of
being monogamous when they take the vows, it doesn't mean
they won't change their thinking at some future time.

Couples need to realize that there's no one-time promise or
event that can guarantee monogamy. Instead, an ongoing process

of honest communication is essential in order for monogamy to be a reality for a lifetime. When there's only a promise of monogamy, there's no way to determine when a person's thinking is changing and they are moving toward the possibility of an affair.

Here are some of the realities about most people who get involved in an affair:

- They weren't looking for an affair
- They didn't intend to have an affair
- They didn't think they were vulnerable to an affair

The fact is that anyone is vulnerable. In fact, people are even more vulnerable when they think they're immune just because they don't intend to have an affair. This is particularly true when it comes to workplace affairs, emotional affairs, or affairs that begin on the Internet.

Many people who never intended to have an affair fail to take steps necessary to prevent it from happening. For instance, the first red flag is when thoughts or feelings about someone else are kept secret. The very process of keeping the feelings secret tends to make them stronger. It allows for focusing only on the positive aspects and blinds people to the reality of the consequences of acting on the feelings.

So talking about it (in whatever way can bring it into reality without creating additional problems) can help cut through the fantasy. This "talking" can be with a professional or a friend or family member who can be totally trusted. There's something about discussing your thinking out loud (and seeing it through the eyes of someone else) that allows you to view it more realistically.

An interesting (and provocative) approach to reframing the way we assume monogamy was presented by Adam Phillips in his book titled *Monogamy*. Here's an excerpt from that book: *"Infidelity is such a problem because we take monogamy for granted; we treat it as the norm. Perhaps we should take infidelity for granted, assume it with unharassed ease. Then we would be able to think about monogamy."*

One of my goals in writing this book on preventing affairs is to encourage people to really think about monogamy, not just assume it.

Survey Results for "Taking the marriage vows seriously and intending to be faithful"

Ranked #2 out of the 16 items on the list

52.6 percent of total respondents chose this among their top 5 items

All percentages below reflect how many respondents chose this among their top 5 items.

There were only slight differences between women and men.

51 percent of women

58 percent of men

There were also only slight differences between those who are married and those who are single.

53 percent of marrieds

44 percent of singles

But there was a much greater difference between those who had personal experience with affairs and those without such experience.

49 percent of those with personal experience (ranked #3 by this sub-group)

63 percent of those with no experience (co-ranked #1 by this sub-group)

This continues a pattern where those without personal experience tend to think their "beliefs" about the importance of various factors will be more of a deterrent than has been the experience of those with personal experience.

Comments about Results for "Vows"

The fact that "vows" ranked second in preventing affairs (out of the entire list of 16 items) indicates a high degree of reliance on this one act in preventing affairs. It's interesting that such a high percentage of all groups chose this item, particularly considering the evidence (as reflected in the high divorce rate) that the vows do not carry the kind of protection for the marriage that most people hope or assume. Therefore, the strong belief that "taking the marriage vows seriously and intending to be faithful" will prevent affairs over the course of the marriage is not warranted.

Expectations vs. Reality

When a couple take their vows, they clearly intend to keep them. But that intention was not based on having made a careful assessment of just what the vows mean—and what's needed in order to keep them. The vows are such an integral part of the wedding ceremony that they're likely to be taken for granted rather than being analyzed and discussed. Even when couples write their own vows rather than repeating the formal vows, there's still a certain level of naïveté in believing that the words (however heartfelt at the time) will sustain their commitment over time. The true strength of the commitment comes not from having spoken the vows; it comes from actually living them day in and day out.

This means couples can't just assume that saying the vows at the wedding will somehow magically keep them committed to those promises throughout the life of the marriage. They need to spend more time thinking about and talking about the meaning behind the vows on an ongoing basis.

Like most things related to a long-term marriage, no one-time statement or one-time intention is sufficient to sustain a marriage as people change through the years. It's essential to invest time and energy into the commitment implied by the vows—rather than relying on the words spoken at the wedding ceremony. It's unreasonable to expect the vows to be central to long-term protection from affairs.

The Bottom Line about "Vows"

A belief that the vows will somehow protect you from affairs places far too much of a burden on this one act, and, unfortunately, it means that people may fail to take other steps that might be more effective in preventing affairs.

Regardless of how seriously the vows are taken, they only reflect the feelings at that time; however, people change throughout a long-term marriage. In fact, the high percentage of divorces (still around 50 percent of all marriages) is clear evidence of the unreliability of counting on the vows as protection from affairs. In other words, if the vows don't protect from divorce, there's no reason to believe they offer protection from affairs. In fact, some people who wouldn't actually get a divorce would (and do) have affairs.

So intending to be faithful is a great starting place. (For instance, entering marriage without this intention might make affairs inevitable.) But the belief needs to be reinforced on an ongoing basis by actions that reflect the continuing commitment to this intention.

Recommitment: repeating/renewing the marriage vows

Some couples who believe their wedding vows are significant in preventing affairs may think that having a renewal ceremony will provide the kind of insurance they are seeking. However, these couples are in the minority—as evidenced by the fact that the item "taking the marriage vows seriously" was ranked #2 while "repeating the vows" came in last in the rankings.

When there has not been an affair in the marriage, a recommitment ceremony may be a nice gesture—just for a couple to remind each other of their continuing commitment to the marriage. It may be a kind of celebration of the positive state of the relationship at that time. But it has no more power to prevent affairs than the initial vows.

The consideration of a recommitment ceremony is more likely to happen when there has already been an incident of breaking the initial vows, as a symbol of a renewed effort to "get it right" this time. But, again, it's not a meaningful indicator of the degree to which monogamy is now assured. A commitment to honesty and to engaging in other ongoing actions has a far greater impact on maintaining a monogamous marriage.

Survey Results for "Repeating/renewing the marriage vows"

Ranked #16 out of the 16 items on the list

3 percent of total respondents chose this among their top 5 items

The percentages below reflect how many respondents chose this among their top 5 items.

3 percent of women
3 percent of men

4 percent of all respondents with experience
2 percent of all respondents with no experience

Comments about Results for "Recommitment"

This item ranked last out of the 16 items presented. This is not surprising, since it's obvious that if the initial vows don't protect against affairs, a renewal of the vows is not likely to do so.

In fact, having had experience with affairs seems to be the primary basis for this item's consideration—since "recommitment" was chosen by twice as many respondents with personal experience as those with no experience (4 percent vs. 2 percent).

The Bottom Line about "Recommitment"

There is no magic in repeating the vows. Assigning too much significance to the idea of a recommitment ceremony tends to put far more emphasis on the symbols of our commitment than on the actions that demonstrate that commitment.

Another event that is more symbol than substance is the importance often placed on what happens (or fails to happen) on Valentine's Day. Just as whatever is said or done on Valentine's Day is not an accurate reflection of the actual state of the relationship, neither is "renewing the marriage vows." In other words, just as the vows expressed at the initial wedding ceremony are not sufficient to guarantee the future, a recommitment ceremony is also not a guarantee.

Most people would prefer to be able to get this settled once and for all, but dealing with the issue of monogamy is an ongoing process, not something that can be established on the basis of one discussion or one promise. The best way to prevent affairs is not by making a promise of monogamy, but by making a commitment to honesty.

Frankly, if and when there is a recommitment ceremony, it's highly recommended that the commitment be made to "honesty" rather than just repeating the vows, promising to be faithful. That's because the actions involved in communicating with honesty show tangible evidence of a commitment to the marriage far beyond any one-time (or repeated) vow to be monogamous.

Chapter 6

• • • • • •

Having children together and being a devoted mother/father

The belief that having children can prevent affairs is similar to the thinking that having children will "help the marriage." Most couples want to have children and pursue this path, but while children may significantly enrich a marriage, they also can be a source of friction and other problems.

As stated by Esther Perel in her book *Mating in Captivity*, *"Children are a blessing, a delight, a wonder. They're also a minor cataclysm."* Unfortunately, most couples are so caught up in the excitement of becoming parents that they ignore the severe disruption to "life as they knew it" before becoming parents.

The enormous time and energy involved in being a "devoted mother or father" can leave almost no room for spending time or energy on each other—or even on yourself. The children can become the center of a couple's world, crowding out almost everything else. And one of the first and most obvious changes is that sex is likely to be severely diminished, often becoming almost non-existent during the early years of bearing and raising children.

While this chapter focuses on having children, it is closely connected with changes in having sex (or not having sex). For most new mothers, sex is the last thing on their minds. Her focus is almost exclusively on the child's well-being and on her own sense of being overwhelmed with all the demands on her time and energy. Since mothers are the ones who give birth and are most often the ones doing more of the early parenting, they have little time or patience for what feels like demands from their husbands.

And a husband may feel left out and/or jealous of the time and attention his wife is paying to the child while mostly ignoring him. Unfortunately, this dynamic can make a husband somewhat more vulnerable to an affair.

It's particularly sad (but not particularly unusual) to hear that a husband's affair began while his wife was pregnant or preoccupied with the care of an infant. Naturally, this is seen by the wife as a double-whammy—since he's emotionally unavailable at the very time she needs him most.

Of course, it's not just when the children are infants that they may dominate the lives of their parents. As the child gets older (and perhaps other siblings come along), the initial strain can become a way of life. In today's child-centered society, the children and their activities often take center stage in the life of the family, leaving little time or energy for pursuing couple activities. Over the years, this pattern of putting the children first is not only detrimental to the couple relationship, but ultimately detrimental to the development of a child who grows up to believe that the world completely revolves around him/her.

After many years of parenting, many couples begin to see each other more in their role of mother or father than as husband and wife. In fact, it's not unusual to hear older couples (after having raised their children) refer to each other not by name but by these roles—calling each other Mother or Father, even when no one else is around.

Survey Results for "Having children together and being a devoted mother/father"

Ranked #14 out of the 16 items on the list

6.6 percent of total respondents chose this among their top 5 items

All percentages below reflect how many respondents chose this among their top 5 items.

Men choose this item in greater numbers than women by a wide margin (more than twice as often).

5 percent of women

13 percent of men

A comparison of married women with no experience and married men with no experience again shows that men chose this item more often—in about the same ratio as the totals of women and men.

7 percent of married women with no experience

18 percent of married men with no experience

Married men with *no* experience see this item as much more significant than married men with personal experience.

9 percent of married men with experience

18 percent of married men with no experience

Comments about Results for "Children"

Although the percentages choosing this item were low, they are quite revealing. While the assumption might be that mothers would rank this item higher, it's clear from the responses that men see "having children" as a far greater prevention factor than do women. The reason for this may be that if an affair leads to the dissolution of the marriage, it's the man who is most likely to lose daily contact with his children. So with the potential consequences of an affair being greater for men, this practical factor takes on more significance.

Looking more closely at the breakdowns is also revealing, particularly the responses of married men with no experience when compared both with married women with no experience and with married men who did have experience. Based on these comparisons, "being a devoted father" seems to be one of the factors that prevented affairs among those married men who had *not* had an affair.

While most parents will say that their children are the most important people in their lives, their actions do not bear this out. And on some level, there seems to be a recognition that this concern is more an ideal than a reality—based on the fact that "children" was ranked #13 out of the 16 items.

The Bottom Line about "Children"

For those who believe that a devoted parent (particularly a mother) wouldn't do anything that might hurt the kids, this is more an ideal than a reality. Being devoted to the kids doesn't preclude having an affair.

In fact, many men become more vulnerable to affairs when their wives transfer much of their emotional investment from them to the children, actually pitting husbands against the children for their wives' time, love and attention. As the bond between mother and child continues to strengthen, many men are left feeling "less important" in the family and more vulnerable to praise and attention from other women.

Likewise, women who begin to see themselves (and to be seen by their husbands) primarily in their role of "mother" may be more vulnerable to praise and attention from other men. Also, some women who might otherwise divorce stay married "for the sake of the kids"—and have an affair on the side.

Unfortunately, "being a devoted mother or father" doesn't necessarily preclude their pursuits as an individual, regardless of whether those pursuits are work, social activities, hobbies—or affairs.

Chapter 7

• • • • • •

Concerns about consequences: hurting others, getting caught

In addition to the factors involved in preventing affairs that are based on either "beliefs" or "actions," there are also some practical concerns about "consequences" that can't be ignored. While these do not carry the same weight as other factors, they do play a role and need to be considered—since preventing affairs depends on a combination of many factors.

This chapter focuses on two possible "concerns about consequences":

- Being concerned about hurting your partner and children
- Being afraid of getting caught, risking possible divorce

The respondents to the questionnaire ranked these items generally lower than other factors. And, indeed, these factors do seem to play a less significant role in preventing affairs. As difficult as it may be to imagine, many people involved in affairs simply don't pause to consider the possibility of facing consequences.

The reason consequences have so little effect is that those involved in affairs usually make a point of ignoring, denying, or rationalizing the repercussions of their actions. Actually, ignoring

49

the potential impact of these factors is an integral part of having an affair. To consciously focus on potential consequences would be to diminish the willingness to act on this impulse.

No matter how dire the consequences might be, they seem to have little effect. Evidence of this is the fact that when AIDS first came on the scene, people assumed this concern would significantly decrease the number of affairs. But that has not been the case. That's because this fear just gets tucked away alongside all the other potential consequences as something that is ignored, denied, or rationalized by those engaged in an affair.

Nevertheless, we want to take a quick look at two of these practical factors—*focusing primarily on the responses to the Questionnaire.*

Survey Results for "Being concerned about hurting your partner and children"

Ranked #9 out of the 16 items on the list

32.3 percent of total respondents chose this among their top 5 items

All percentages below reflect how many respondents chose this among their top 5 items.

Slightly more women than men ranked this item in their top 5

34 percent of women

28 percent of men

There was no significant difference in comparisons based on being married or single.

32 percent of all marrieds

33 percent of all singles

There was no significant difference in comparisons based or whether or not someone had personal experience. In fact, this item received the most uniform responses of any item on the list.

33 percent of all with personal experience

30 percent of all with no experience

Comments about Results for "Hurt"

While "hurt" was ranked #9 out of 16 items, this concern is not reflected in the actions of those having affairs. Any thought that might be given to the possible pain is often dealt with by denial. In fact, the classic way of thinking among people having affairs is *"What he/she doesn't know won't hurt him/her."* The way this rationalization works goes something like...*"No one will find out, so no one will get hurt."* But, as all those who have been hurt by a spouse's affair know, they usually do suspect and/or find out and it does hurt—a lot!

And the children get hurt as well. The stress experienced by the parents in dealing with the fallout from the affair has a carryover effect on the children, whether the marriage is rebuilt or ends in divorce. And if the affair leads to divorce, the impact on children can be devastating.

The Bottom Line about "Hurt"

If having an affair were based on rational thinking and clear decision-making, there would be a strong focus on the risk of hurting your partner and/or children. However, affairs are almost completely based on emotion, shutting out the rational thinking that could make a difference.

In most instances, people don't decide to have an affair in the way you might decide to take a certain job or live in a certain area. As discussed earlier, once people start down the road toward an affair, they tend to block out any practical considerations that might stop (or even slow down) this pursuit.

Survey Results for "Being afraid of getting caught, risking possible divorce"

Ranked #13 out of the 16 items on the list

7.3 percent of total respondents chose this among their top 5 items

All percentages below reflect how many respondents chose this among their top 5 items.

6 percent of women

10 percent of men

Differences based on gender

Men chose this item more often than women—whether or not they had personal experience.

7 percent of married women with experience

13 percent of married men with experience

3 percent of married women with no experience

7 percent of married men with no experience

Differences based on experience

Both women with experience and men with experience chose it more often than women or men without personal experience. (The differences based on experience mirror those based on gender.)

7 percent of married women with experience

3 percent of married women with no experience

13 percent of married men with experience

7 percent of married men with no experience

Comments about Results for "Fear"

The #13 ranking out of 16 items shows that people don't think "being afraid of getting caught" or "risking possible divorce" is much of a preventative. These results are borne out by experience in that I've seen through the years that people having affairs are usually in complete denial of the risks they're taking.

The Bottom Line about "Fear"

When a person discovers their spouse's affair, in struggling to understand how this could have happened, they inevitably ask the practical question of how their mate could have taken the *risks*: the risk of getting caught, the risk of a venereal disease, the risk of pregnancy, the risk of divorce.

As difficult as it may be to comprehend, in most cases the person having an affair simply doesn't think about these risks. They just assume nothing will ever go wrong. Even the added risk of AIDS didn't have a significant impact on people having affairs; they simply ignore this risk in the same way they ignore all the others.

Affairs are extremely exciting for most people, a heady experience that exists outside the normal distractions of life's problems. And this excitement simply blocks out the focus on whatever risks might be involved. To focus on the risks and the fears of repercussions would be to interfere with the pleasure of the affair. So they simply ignore the elephant in the room.

Rationally, it may seem impossible to understand how people could fail to consider the risks and consequences, but having an affair is not a rational act. It's impulse-driven and is guided by emotions, not by reason.

The bottom line is that the reason "fear" doesn't act as a deterrent is the same as the reason "hurt" doesn't carry much weight. In both instances, people are in denial about the possibility of getting caught, so they never contemplate the repercussions that could lead to divorce.

Chapter 8

••••••

Having no opportunity—no free time, never travel, etc.

One fact about extramarital affairs is that it's an equal opportunity activity. In an earlier era, there may have been some truth to the idea that having an affair required some special circumstances to make it possible. (This thinking gave rise to the common jokes about traveling salesmen.) However, those days of limited opportunity are long gone—if they ever existed.

In today's environment, it's almost impossible to find situations where there could be absolutely *no* opportunity. Granted, some situations may make it easier than others; but the truth is reflected by the old saying, "Where there's a will, there's a way."

In fact, having the will to have an affair is not even required. Many (most?) affairs are not premeditated; people simply allow them to happen—for a variety of reasons. One of the most common places of opportunity for affairs is the workplace (which will be discussed in Chapter 13). For instance, working late and long lunches easily overcome the barriers to having "no free time."

Another prime area of opportunity is the Internet (which will be discussed in Chapter 14). The idea that "never traveling" means there's a lack of opportunity has been rendered irrelevant in the day of sitting in front of a computer anywhere in the world and connecting with someone on a personal basis.

So it should be of no comfort to think that your spouse is too busy to have an affair—or that he/she never travels and is always home at night.

Survey Results for "Having no opportunity—no free time, never travel, etc."

Ranked #15 out of the 16 items on the list

5.4 percent of total respondents chose this among their top 5 items

All percentages below reflect how many respondents chose this among their top 5 items.

Although this item was seen as significant by a very small percentage of people, the results produced one of the most striking differences in perspective between different groups.

7 percent of women

1 percent of men

5 percent of marrieds

11 percent of singles

Comments about Results for "Opportunity"

Singles chose this item more than twice as often as marrieds, indicating that those who are married recognize that there's always the possibility of an affair, despite no obvious "opportunity"—while those who are single are basing their opinion on trying to envision what circumstances might be required to make an affair possible.

A further assessment of the breakdown for this item showed that the 1 percent of men choosing this item were men who had no experience. And zero percent of the 104 married men with personal experience saw lack of opportunity as a primary deterrent—which would indicate that there's always an "opportunity" if you want to find one.

The Bottom Line about "Opportunity"

In a much earlier period it was assumed that affairs happened mostly among people who traveled, i.e. the jokes about traveling salesmen. Salesmen, truckers, entertainers, professional athletes, and others who travel extensively were considered prime candidates. And those whose spouses didn't fit that profile breathed a sigh of relief. In fact, while traveling may make them easier to hide, affairs are certainly not restricted to those who travel.

There is still an assumption among many people that if their spouse works very long hours and/or is home every night that there's not much opportunity. However, the significant increase in work-related affairs is evidence of the fact that there is a great deal of opportunity in the workplace. And, of course, the Internet has also made opportunity a reality for almost everyone.

Since "lack of opportunity" is an extremely small factor in preventing affairs, it's imperative that couples not be lulled into thinking their particular life circumstances will keep them "safe."

Part II

What WILL Work
(Focusing on Actions and Behaviors)

A person's actions and behaviors (regardless of their attitudes or beliefs about monogamy) are far more significant factors in preventing affairs through the years. The nature of the need to continuously work at maintaining monogamy is reflected in the initial premise presented in the Introduction:

> *Preventing affairs is not like having a one-time inoculation or even getting occasional booster shots. It's more like taking a pill every day for the rest of your life.*

Each of the seven chapters in Part II focuses on an item in the Questionnaire related to an ongoing *action* or a *behavior* that helps prevent affairs. These include:

Having ongoing honest communication about all marital issues

Acknowledging and discussing attractions to others

Trying to meet your partner's needs

Having a satisfying marital sex life

Maintaining professional boundaries with co-workers

Avoiding personal relationships on the Internet

The bottom line

Chapter 9

• • • • • •

Having ongoing honest communication about all marital issues

Honesty is the single most important factor in preventing affairs.
All too often, when we think of "honesty," we think of brutal
honesty (unloading or dumping our negative feelings). For
instance, if someone says, "Can I be perfectly honest?"... you
know that the next words out of their mouth are likely to be
some kind of criticism.

Part of the reason for this view of honesty is because of the
kind of honesty that became prevalent in the 60s with "saying it
like it is" and "letting it all hang out." This led many people to
see honesty as thoughtlessly hurting each other with bluntness,
which in turn led to excusing dishonesty as tact and kindness
toward others. This is a narrow, shortsighted view of honesty and
a naïve view of dishonesty.

However, "responsible honesty" is an entirely different
matter. Responsible honesty is a special kind of honesty that is
undertaken specifically for the purpose of building a stronger
bond through sharing who you really are so you can fully know
each other. And within that framework, you can talk about
absolutely anything!

Most people like to think of themselves as honest, but they're
likely to be defining "honest" in a narrow way as simply "not

lying." You've probably heard the lyrics of the song: "Ask me no questions, I'll tell you no lies." However, honesty is much more than just "not lying"; it's "not *withholding* relevant information."

To clarify, "not withholding relevant information" doesn't mean sharing every single thought. That's not possible, even if it were desirable. But it *is* possible to make a point of not withholding information that is relevant to the relationship. By this standard, most of us are far from honest.

There's a tendency to think of honesty only as telling something that was previously kept secret. But the main power of honesty is in sharing feelings. When a couple share their deepest feelings about everything, including the scary stuff (like attractions to other people or fears of their spouse having an affair), they develop a deeper understanding of each other.

Many people think that talking about such emotional issues will inevitably cause problems. But it's far more likely that it will lead to a closer relationship because of the comfort involved in feeling you will be told the truth about anything that comes up.

It's ironic that while honesty is recognized as important to a relationship, most people also fear it and see it as a risk to the security of the relationship. Unfortunately, people haven't appreciated how much risk is involved in dishonesty. They typically focus only on the risks they fear in being more honest—and this is particularly true when it comes to discussing sexual issues. But in my many years of working with the issue of extramarital affairs, it's clear that the benefits of "responsible honesty" far outweigh any potential risk.

Excuses for Dishonesty

Of course, despite the persuasive arguments for the benefits of pursuing honesty, people tend to resist and come up with a lot of excuses for dishonesty.

"I don't want to hurt his or her feelings."

Protecting the other person is probably the most common reason given for being dishonest. No doubt this is a genuine motive in some cases. In others, it's a rationalization. We need to ask ourselves: Are we really thinking of the other person or are we protecting ourselves from having to deal with their reaction to the truth? Even if our motives are pure, there's still a chance that our secrecy will eventually do them more harm than telling the truth.

"He/she doesn't want to know the truth."

Much of the time this is an assumption that's never checked out. It's especially convenient to assume this when we aren't personally prepared to deal with the truth. This assumption by one person often leads to an unspoken agreement by both of them to be dishonest as the relationship ages. Neither partner thinks of it as being dishonest—it's just being practical and respecting each other's wishes.

"Some things are better off not discussed—just kept to yourself."

This serves to avoid problems for a while, but it doesn't solve anything. In fact, it usually makes things worse. The number of topics you can't discuss grows like a cancer—until there's very little meaningful conversation left. The results of this kind of alienation are easy to detect if you pay attention to the way couples relate to each other when they're eating out in a restaurant. It's not difficult to tell which couples are married just by watching them for a while. When there's no conversation, it's a pretty good clue that they're married and just don't have anything to say to each other. They've probably long since ceased to share anything but the most practical aspects of life. They may have accumulated so many hurts and resentments through the years that they find it safer and more comfortable to say nothing.

"What purpose would be served by pointing out all his or her faults?"

Responsible honesty is *not* about criticism; in fact, it's not about describing the other person in any way. It's about disclosing yourself.

The common element in all these excuses is the idea that it's not reasonable or possible to develop full, open honesty. In fact, the idea of being completely honest may seem so unrealistic and unachievable for most people that they may feel there's no point in even trying to be honest.

However, developing honesty is a process, not an event. And the goal for each couple (which is certainly attainable) is to gradually *increase* their level of honesty.

How to Communicate Honestly

It's not enough to just arbitrarily decide to be honest without laying the proper groundwork. Without establishing a framework, your honesty can be misinterpreted and even damaging to the relationship. I alluded to this earlier in defining "responsible honesty" in terms of its being specifically for the purpose of building a stronger bond.

This means that you sit down as a couple and establish this understanding of your commitment to honesty. You acknowledge the danger of secrecy and agree to share your deepest thoughts on an ongoing basis, including the scary thoughts that might involve attractions or other potential threats to the marriage.

However, it's not enough to just agree in theory; you need to specifically discuss what it would mean to the two of you as a couple if one of you were to have an affair. This does not involve issuing threats or giving ultimatums. It does mean honestly sharing the likely impact on the thoughts and feelings of each of you if this were to happen.

Being armed with this kind of specific focus on the potential ramifications of an affair brings a sense of reality to the consequences. This may help undermine the typical pattern where people tempted to have an affair completely ignore any consequences. Ignoring the fallout from an affair would be much more difficult if there had been honest discussions about the pain and devastation an affair would bring to all concerned.

Survey Results for "Having ongoing honest communication about all marital issues"

Ranked #1 out of the 16 items on the list

79.3 percent of total respondents chose this among their top 5 items.

All percentages below reflect how many respondents chose this among their top 5 items.

82 percent of women

72 percent of men

Honesty was ranked #1 in every subcategory except married men with no experience, who ranked it #3 behind "morals" and "vows." (It was impossible to factor in the responses of single men for this or any other item, since only 3 of the 755 respondents were single men.)

In all categories, a higher percentage of those with personal experience chose "honesty" than those with no experience.

87 percent of married women with experience

65 percent of married women with no experience

80 percent of married men with experience

60 percent of married men with no experience

82 percent of single women with experience

62 percent of single women with no experience

Comments about Results for "Honesty"

The significant result that immediately pops out is the overwhelming consensus on the *importance* of honesty. While it's understandable that those who've already dealt with affairs have a stronger appreciation for the value of "honesty," the good news is that even those without personal experience still ranked it #1 (albeit at a somewhat smaller percentage) in all categories except married men with no personal experience.

The results continue to reflect the fairly consistent pattern with most of the items—where those who've had personal experience possess additional insight and perspective due to their experience. Everyone seems to recognize the importance of "honesty" in the abstract, but it becomes very concrete once people have had personal experience in dealing with an affair.

Another clear difference is reflected by the choices based on gender, where in every category a higher percentage of women chose "honesty" than did men. This is not surprising, given the way women are generally more comfortable talking about relationship issues. But it's a positive sign that despite men's general reluctance to "talk about the relationship," they nevertheless have a strong appreciation for the importance of honesty.

Cultural Differences Regarding Honesty

I want to acknowledge that different cultures and sub-cultures have different attitudes and beliefs about secrecy and disclosure, etc. And although I've had my website since 1996 and hear from people around the world, my primary audience is in the U.S. and my own experience is based on living in the U.S.

So this cultural perspective is reflected in the results about "honesty."

The Bottom Line about "Honesty"

Honesty is the single most important factor in preventing affairs. In fact, dishonesty and deception are essential components of having an affair, allowing affairs to flourish.

No one can be absolutely positive that their partner would *never* have an affair, so it's critical to communicate about this issue. Most people have all kinds of private fears that they're afraid to confront. They look for "signals" or try to find meaning in various actions (or inactions). But it's far better to *know* what your partner is thinking than to guess, and honesty is by far the best path to achieving this goal.

You can't overestimate the significance of establishing a strong commitment to "responsible honesty"—which, as mentioned earlier, means "not withholding *relevant* information." (Having an extramarital affair is certainly relevant to the marriage.)

Not only is it important to be honest about temptations; but if an affair does take place, it's critical to reveal it "sooner rather than later." Suspicions and questions won't just go away by being ignored, deflected or criticized; that kind of response only intensifies the fear—and the "need to know." In fact, the denial that is so common when questioned about an affair only serves to make it much more devastating when the truth finally comes out—as it most likely will. It also makes it more difficult to recover and rebuild trust.

Regardless of whatever reasons or excuses may be offered as to why someone might have an affair, the essential "trump card" is being willing to be dishonest and deceptive. In the final analysis (regardless of the reason for *wanting* to have an affair), acting on that desire ultimately depends on a lack of honesty. So a commitment to honesty is inherently significant in preventing affairs.

Chapter 10

· · · · · ·

Acknowledging and discussing attractions to others

When you first start getting serious (and perhaps jealous and possessive), you're likely to make it clear that you don't like it if your partner indicates any attraction to someone else. Even though you may realize it's natural for your partner (and for you) to find others attractive, it's probably something you don't want to think about. You'd like to believe it won't happen, so you may convince yourself that somehow your relationship will be different.

However, if you try to deny the possibility of attractions, you send a subtle (or not so subtle) signal to your partner that you don't want to know about any of their feelings of attraction toward others. Since attractions are both normal and inevitable, you're in essence sending a message that says, *"Lie to me; pretend you're never attracted to anyone else."* This, of course, causes other problems related to honesty that can have serious consequences for your relationship.

Accepting the reality of attractions to others is the first step toward being able to keep them in perspective. If you see attractions as a direct threat to your love (thinking that if your partner loved you they would never be attracted to anyone else), you're granting power to attractions that they would not otherwise possess.

Attractions are not, in and of themselves, a problem. The problem comes when they are acted on. And the best way to decrease the likelihood of that happening is to honestly discuss this issue and your feelings about it on an ongoing basis.

Attractions become a much greater threat to the relationship whenever acknowledging them is taboo. If you can't talk about these feelings, they become your own private secret and are likely to grow in intensity and desire. But openly discussing your feelings brings a degree of reality to the issue that leads to a more sensible and responsible way of thinking, which in turn reduces the desire to act on the attractions. So talk honestly about your attractions and how to deal with them in order to reduce their power and effect.

This concept is also reflected in Esther Perel's book *Mating in Captivity*: *"Some couples choose not to ignore the lure of the forbidden. Instead, they subvert its power... [They] have chosen to acknowledge the possibility of the third...inviting the third goes some way toward containing its volatility, not to mention its appeal. It is no longer a shadow but a presence, something to talk about openly...When we can tell the truth safely, we are less inclined to keep secrets."*

Couples tend to think it's too risky to openly discuss such things, but the greater risk is in *not* discussing them, which allows the attractions to grow. The secrecy allows a person to focus *only* on a positive fantasy—while talking openly about how to deal with attractions leads to also focusing on the risks of acting on them.

So it's important for couples to talk about their attractions to others—and more importantly, to talk about how they will deal with those attractions or temptations. While it's definitely the wiser course of action to talk about attractions instead of either denying them or keeping them secret, there's still the issue of learning how to go about acknowledging attractions without keeping emotions constantly stirred up and jealousy flaring.

You can't reasonably expect to have these kinds of discussions unless you make a clear commitment to responsible honesty—which in this instance means honestly discussing attractions for the specific purpose of preventing the attractions from getting out of hand.

Hiding attractions can be the first step toward hiding temptations, then hiding actions. So avoiding this first deception also avoids having the attraction escalate into temptation and action.

In addition to helping prevent affairs, talking about attractions can draw you closer together and allow you to know each other better. Unfortunately, many couples cease to know each other after years of withholding their private thoughts from one another. And the distance created by this lack of sharing opens up possibilities for all kinds of secrets and the problems they can bring.

Survey Results for "Acknowledging and discussing attractions to others"

Ranked #8 out of the 16 items on the list

34.2 percent of total respondents chose this among their top 5 items

All percentages below reflect how many respondents chose this among their top 5 items.

Females ranked it #5, while males ranked it #11. Clearly, women are much more attuned to the risks associated with failing to discuss (and deal with) attractions to others.

38 percent of women
23 percent of men

Those with experience ranked "attractions" #4; those without personal experience ranked it #11.

44 percent of married women with experience
17 percent of married women with no experience

29 percent of married men with experience
15 percent of married men with experience

Comments about Results for "Attractions"

Women placed more importance on "talking about attractions" than did men. This is not surprising—since it's consistent with the way women place more importance on honesty in terms of "talking about the relationship." And "talking about attractions" is just a more specific focus in talking about the relationship.

However, the more striking differences were between those (both women and men) with personal experience as compared to those *without* personal experience. This shows a continuation of the fact that firsthand experience allows people to have a clearer sense of what does or doesn't make a difference in preventing affairs.

The Bottom Line about "Attractions"

The fact that your partner *looks* at others (and perhaps is attracted to others) is not, in and of itself, a problem; in fact, it's natural to be attracted to others. The problem comes if the attractions are acted on. And the best way to decrease the likelihood of that happening is to honestly discuss this issue and your feelings about it on an ongoing basis.

If you can't tell your partner when you find someone attractive, you won't tell them when you're tempted to act on that attraction, and you certainly won't tell them if and when you do take any action.

A couple's best hope for monogamy lies in rejecting the idea that they can *assume* monogamy without discussing the issue, or that they can *assure* monogamy by making threats as to what they would do if it happened. Either of these paths creates a cycle of dishonesty.

In either case, people don't feel free to admit being attracted to someone else. The effect on the relationship is to cause it to be filled with jealousy and suspicion, as well as making it *less* likely that it will be monogamous.

But if both partners realize that attractions to others are likely (indeed inevitable) no matter how much they love each other, they can engage in ongoing honest communication about the reality of the temptations and how to avoid the consequences of *acting* on those temptations. The effect on the relationship is to create a sense of closeness and a knowledge of each other that replaces suspicion with trust, making it *more* likely to be monogamous.

While this should not be taken as a license to be gross or crude or embarrassing, couples do need to be able to talk candidly and realistically about this whole issue in order to prevent the very thing they fear.

Effectively dealing with attractions involves:
1. Accepting that attractions to others are normal and inevitable, no matter how much you love each other.
2. Talking honestly about your attractions and how to deal with them in order to reduce their power and effect.
3. Being aware of the dangers in acting on your attractions.

Chapter 11

• • • • • •

Trying to meet your partner's needs

A common reason (excuse?) for affairs is that my partner didn't "meet my needs." This is ludicrous—in that no one person can meet all of another person's needs.

The desire to meet each other's needs is one of the most important features of a good relationship. But to be of real benefit, this effort (by both parties) will spring freely from love, not from fear that a failure to do so will lead our partner to have an affair. The fact is that we can't control another person's behavior by our actions; each of us is responsible for our own behavior.

Since all marriages have problems from time to time, it's easy to point a finger (after the fact) to any unmet needs or other identifiable problems in the relationship—and say *that's* why the affair happened. However, if that particular problem hadn't existed, there would have been some other problem—and that one would have been identified as the reason for the affair.

Here's an example of how this works: One woman blamed herself for her husband's affair, saying, *"I was a career woman who wasn't paying enough attention to him—and he needed a homebody who devoted herself to him in a way I failed to do."* Another woman blamed herself, saying, *"I was a full-time homemaker who was boring to him because I wasn't 'out in the world'—and he needed a career woman who brought the excitement that I failed to provide."*

So while unmet needs may be a quick and easy excuse, it's not the reason people have affairs. In fact, there's no *one* reason why someone has an affair; affairs are the result of a combination of three broad *sets* of factors, including:

1. Factors that *push* people into affairs
   (problems, faults, shortcomings, etc.)

2. Factors that *pull* people into affairs
   (excitement, novelty, curiosity, etc.)

3. Societal factors
   (fascination/glamorization of affairs, marketing of sex, secrecy)

1. Some factors that *push* people toward affairs:
   • Desire to escape or find relief from a painful relationship
   • Boredom
   • Desire to fill gaps in an existing relationship
   • Desire to punish one's partner
   • Need to prove one's attractiveness or worth
   • Desire for attention

2. Some factors that *pull* people toward affairs:
   • Attraction: sex, companionship, admiration, power
   • Novelty
   • Excitement, risk, or challenge
   • Curiosity
   • Enhanced self-image
   • Falling in love

3. Some of the many societal factors:
   • Affairs are glamorized in movies, soap operas, romance novels, and TV shows of all kinds. Disclosure of public

figures having affairs is headline news because we're fascinated and titillated by hearing of others' affairs.

- People are bombarded with images of women as sex objects in advertising and marketing campaigns. Over and over, the message to men is that the good life includes a parade of sexy women in their lives, leading them to seek to fulfill this fantasy. And women inadvertently buy into the idea of projecting a sexy image, leading them to be more vulnerable to having an affair.
- The lack of good sex education and the existence of sexual taboos combine to make it difficult for most partners to talk honestly about sex.
- As teenagers we get conditioned in deception when it comes to sex—engaging in sexual activity while hiding it from our parents.
- The "code of secrecy" about affairs is a major factor— because it provides protection for the person having affairs and leads them to believe they won't get caught.

Athough affairs are caused by a combination of factors from all three of these categories, most people continue to place far too much emphasis on the *push* factors (like not having your needs met) than is warranted. I have been promoting this more comprehensive understanding of the reasons for affairs since *The Monogamy Myth* was first published in 1989, but it's only been in recent years that others are expressing the same sentiment.

For instance, Esther Perel's book *Mating in Captivity* includes this observation: *"I question the widespread view that infidelity is always a symptom of deeper problems in a relationship. Affairs are motivated by myriad forces; not all of them are directly related to flaws in the marriage."*

Survey Results for "Trying to meet your partner's needs"

Ranked #5 out of the 16 items on the list

36.3 percent of total respondents chose this among their top 5 items

All percentages below reflect how many respondents chose this among their top 5 items.

More men than women see this item as being significant in preventing affairs.

33 percent of all women

46 percent of all men

Men (with or without personal experience) consistently ranked "needs" higher than it was ranked by women (with or without personal experience).

33 percent of married women with personal experience

48 percent of married men with personal experience

33 percent of married women with *no* personal experience

44 percent of married men with *no* experience

Comments about Results for "Needs"

It's clear that the difference in perception about "needs" is based on gender rather than on personal experience. The most likely basis for men's higher ranking is that men tend to think of their "needs" in terms of *sexual* needs, so it makes sense that men might consider "needs" to be a more significant factor in preventing affairs. It should be noted, however, that affairs are *not* just about sex. We'll focus on "sex" in the next chapter on "having a satisfying marital sex life."

The Bottom Line about "Needs"

All marriages have problems, and after the fact, it easy to go back and identify an "unmet need"—and assign a cause and effect as to why the affair happened. In fact, there is no *one* "problem in the marriage" or *one* reason a person has an affair.

It's always a combination of reasons, including some forces that *push* people toward affairs, some forces that *pull* them toward affairs, and the influence of some general factors in society that contribute to affairs.

Unfortunately, we've tended to think that the *push* factors (especially problems with the marriage) are the only reasons for affairs. And since "failing to meet your partner's needs" is one of the *push* factors, it has been falsely assumed to be a prime reason for affairs.

Of course, the desire to meet each other's needs is an important feature of a good relationship. But to be of real benefit, this effort (by both parties) will spring freely from love, not from fear that a failure to do so will cause our partner to have an affair. The fact is that we can't control another person's behavior by our actions; each of us is responsible for our own behavior.

Chapter 12

· · · · · ·

Having a satisfying marital sex life

Sex is important, but it's not the *most* important aspect of a long-term loving relationship. As has often been pointed out, when a couple's sex life is satisfying, it's a minor part of the relationship; but when it's *not* satisfying, it can become a major source of friction.

However, sexual satisfaction doesn't exist in a vacuum. A critical aspect of dealing with sex in a long-term relationship is establishing whether or not the primary issue is really "sex"—or whether sexual issues are the result of other issues.

For instance, when it comes to differences in preferences about frequency, the lack of interest by one party (more often the woman) can be due to lots of other factors, most notably a lack of trust or a buildup of resentment over feelings of inequity in the relationship.

In fact, after years of marriage most wives have built up a heavy load of resentment about the growing number of issues around which they feel they've done far more sacrificing and accommodating than their husbands. Over time, this can erode loving feelings of all kinds, particularly sexual feelings.

Of course, sex drives do vary; but if a couple genuinely want to find ways to work through the differences to find a mutually satisfying sex life, it can be done.

Sexual compatibility may not come naturally, but there's nothing wrong with getting some professional guidance in learning better ways of dealing with different sexual preferences—if the differences really are strictly sexual. In fact, this is one of the most straightforward issues to deal with, far simpler than the more complicated feelings of fairness, equality, understanding, and commitment. If those things are present in a relationship, no purely sexual differences will stand in the way of finding a way to satisfy both partners in the sexual arena.

Sex in an affair may seem tempting because of the expectation that it will be far more exciting than marital sex. But much of the sexual excitement in an affair is due to the very nature of it being secretive and forbidden, which automatically makes it seem different from "sanctioned" sex in marriage. But the sexual relationship in an affair is not *real* in that it has more to do with acting out a fantasy than with anything about real feelings between real people.

It's not reasonable to compare marital sex with the potential excitement in an affair because that excitement is very superficial and inevitably fades with time—unless a person goes from one affair to another, maintaining the excitement that only comes from constant "newness." So an affair is not a useful sexual standard by which to gauge marital sex.

It's critical to understand that even though marital sex may seem less exciting, it's not less desirable; it's just *different*. It has its own unique form of intensity and excitement, both of which emerge from a deeper connection between you and your spouse.

Eventually, in the best relationships, the best sex is based on the pleasure of full openness to another person without anxiety, uncertainty, or fear. In fact, feeling fully open and connected to another person (in all aspects of your life together) can result in a better sexual relationship than is possible in the momentary excitement from the novelty of sex with someone new.

78

The best sex does not come from "working on it" or "talking about it." It comes from feeling free to be totally open to each other so that you really *know* each other—as each of you shares your hopes, fears, goals, and desires. Intimacy can't be forced. It emerges from the close, trusting, loving feelings that come from caring for the relationship. In moments of true intimacy, you drop the normal boundaries and allow yourself to be known more completely than in any other circumstance. Forging a deep connection based on full honesty with each other and vulnerability to each other allows the sexual feeling to naturally flow as a by-product of that closeness.

With time, experience and practice, a couple develop their own unique sexual style; they learn to function as a good team in reaching a mutual goal of enjoying their sexuality together. This does not come through focusing on certain expectations based on commonly held beliefs about what *should* happen or what others are doing. It's achieved only by approaching your sexual relationship with positive, realistic expectations as to what "good sex" means to the two of you.

Also, this process of constantly learning more about each other (as each person grows and changes) provides a sense of newness that can allow your sex life to be better than any superficial connection with someone else. So the best way to enjoy life-long, exciting sex is not from tricks, spice, or gimmicks, but from really knowing each other on a deep level so you feel free to relax and get in touch with your natural sexual feelings.

Survey Results for "Having a satisfying marital sex life"

Ranked #6 out of the 16 items on the list

35 percent of all total respondents chose this among their top 5 items

All percentages below reflect how many respondents chose this among their top 5 items.

Gender Differences

"Sex" was a far more significant factor for men than for women.

31 percent of women— ranked #9 among all women

48 percent of men— ranked #4 among all men

The difference was even greater between married men with experience and married women with experience.

29 percent of married women with experience ranked it #9

51 percent of married men with experience ranked it #2

Experience Differences: single women *with* and *without* personal experience

Clearly, single women who had affairs with married men were convinced that the affairs were due to lack of sex or unsatisfying sex at home.

23 percent of single women who had *not* had an affair with a married man chose it in their top 5.

73 percent of single women who *had* had an affair with a married man chose it in their top 5.

Marital Differences: married women and single women, both with experience

Whether or not a woman was married seemed to determine her attitude about the importance of "sex" as a cause of affairs. This illustrates the way single women who had affairs with married men believed the affairs were due to the quantity or quality of the sex within the marriage.

Ranked #9 by married women with personal experience

Ranked #2 by single women who had had an affair with a married man

Differences between married men and either married or single women, all with experience

It's clear that married men viewed the importance of "sex" as a cause of affairs differently from either married women (wives) or single women (affair-partners). They saw it as *more* important than wives thought it was, but *less* important than affair-partners believed it to be. Each group of women had the same degree of discrepancy from men's thinking: wives being 22 percent lower and single affair-partners being 22 percent higher.

51 percent of married men

29 percent of married women

73 percent of single women

Comments about Results for "Sex"

This item had the most dramatic differences in responses of any of the 16 items. Of course, it's not surprising that "sex" would be a hot topic in any assessment of factors involved in affairs.

Most of the differences in responses were due to gender and to marital status of respondents. (Note that since only 3 of the 755 respondents were single men, they were not included in the data.)

But the most striking result is the fact that the importance of "sex" was chosen by more single women with personal experience (73 percent) *than any other group*. This 73 percent compares with 23 percent of single women with *no* experience, 29 percent of married women with experience, and even 51 percent of married men with experience.

Differences between Men and Women

Many men who have affairs declare that they still love their wives, but also enjoy the pleasure, excitement, and ego-boost of an affair. If all men were completely honest, many would acknowledge that in their ideal world (where there were no negative consequences and no one got hurt), they would like to have a wife and family—and have affairs too.

This way of thinking is so alien to most women that they can't quite imagine how men can think that way. Women don't see affairs as primarily about "having sex"; they tend to see affairs as being about both sex and love. In fact, married women who have affairs usually convince themselves that they are "in love" with their affair-partner.

Another factor that women have a very hard time understanding is the fact that many men can compartmentalize affairs. Men have been conditioned to be capable of separating sex from other aspects of life in a way that most women can't comprehend. It's crazy-making when men say (as my own husband did): *"My affair had nothing to do with you!"* Huh??? In my mind, it had *everything* to do with me. But he had completely compartmentalized his behavior.

Certainly, not all men compartmentalize to this extent—but many do. It's not so much a "character flaw" as just part of the way men have been conditioned to partition their lives in many areas: work on one hand, home life on the other; rational-thinking on one hand, (blocked) emotions on the other; sex on one hand, love on the other, etc.

The Bottom Line about "Sex"

Sex in an affair may seem tempting because of the expectation that it will be far more exciting than marital sex. But it's not reasonable to compare marital sex with the potential excitement in an affair because that excitement is very superficial and inevitably fades with time—unless a person goes from one affair to another, maintaining the excitement that only comes from constant "newness."

Even though marital sex may *seem* less exciting, it's not less desirable; it's just *different*. It has its own unique form of intensity and excitement, both of which emerge from a deeper connection between you and your spouse.

While sex is important in marital satisfaction (*and* in preventing affairs), it can't be addressed in isolation without recognizing that sexual problems can arise due to dissatisfaction in other areas of the relationship, having nothing to do with sex per se.

Chapter 13

• • • • • •

Maintaining professional boundaries with co-workers

The awareness of the need to avoid workplace affairs is not new. In fact, there's a long list of quite colorful expressions admonishing against affairs at work: *"Don't mix business with pleasure"* and the symbolically male maxims, *"Don't fish off the company pier"* and *"Don't dip your pen in the company ink."*

Nevertheless, many men and women who know and believe in this advice still succumb to workplace affairs. One study reported that 73 percent of men and 42 percent of women meet their extramarital affair-partners at work.

I personally saw the impact of the growing prevalence of workplace affairs back in the 70s and early 80s when I worked as a corporate consultant on male-female issues in the workplace. And in the years since that time, this issue has continued to grow.

But the concern about what happens at work has a long history, beginning with the old stereotype of a man having an affair with his secretary—based on a time when a large percentage of the women in the workforce were secretaries, many of them young and single. For instance, almost all of the women with whom my husband had affairs were women he met through work.

Also, I became aware of this issue at a much earlier time, when I was only 25 years old and working for a man who was much older, very rich and powerful, quite sophisticated—and thought I was wonderful. I became enamored of him, and our ongoing close working relationship created a climate where I became seriously tempted to have an affair. When I saw that I could be tempted, I had to give up my stereotypical thinking about only certain kinds of people becoming involved in affairs. This experience convinced me that *anyone* is vulnerable.

Factors Influencing Affairs at Work

One factor related to the prevalence of workplace affairs is that at work people present a side of themselves that's not representative of the whole person. They're usually committed to looking their best and being on their best behavior.

Another factor is the sheer amount of time and energy spent at work—and the closeness that can develop when people share a commitment to some interesting and/or exciting project (or even possibly share a boredom with a stagnant environment).

When people work together on projects involving large budgets or high stakes, the work environment becomes filled with a sense of vitality and importance, making the office setting a very sexy place. Given this potent atmosphere, it's no wonder that the office has become the most popular source of contact for extramarital affairs. (Note: This is not an "excuse" for affairs; it just helps understand how they can happen.)

The main point is that the workplace offers an environment where there's a shared experience and constant exposure to someone else that's separate from the personal life of spouse and family. So it's one of the most fertile environments for affairs to take hold and become a big problem for everyone concerned.

(Later, I'll focus on the role of others in the workplace who have to deal with the dynamic of workplace affairs.)

Another of the reasons workplace affairs are so common is that when someone becomes aware of others (whether peers or bosses) who are having affairs, it creates an environment where affairs are more likely to happen. When it appears that affairs are the norm (part of the company culture) it contributes to a person's ability to rationalize that *they* could have an affair too. This influence may be so subtle that a person is not even aware of the impact of being exposed to others' actions.

This is *not* to place the blame for an affair on the work environment, only to acknowledge that it's more likely that a person can reconcile the idea of having an affair when in a culture where affairs seem to be happening without serious consequences. Of course, in reality, there are many ramifications of a workplace affair that go beyond risking the marriage to include risking loss of the job, particularly when the affair ends.

Gender Differences in Workplace Affairs

During the years I worked as a corporate consultant, I observed many instances where working relationships became so close that they eventually "crossed the line." I also noticed there were some differences between men and women in relation to their attitude and approach to affairs at work. So I'll address these differences separately, beginning with the men.

Men

Men are often able to compartmentalize their lives and feel that "workplace connections" and "wife and family" have nothing to do with each other. This means there's less of a sense of staying connected to their wives while at work, almost as if they don't exist. This separation of roles makes it easier to block out and ignore the impact of acting on temptations to become involved with other women at work. By the time a man senses what's happening, it's likely to already be well on the way to becoming some kind of a problem.

For instance, a man (despite his lack of intention to do so) could become more involved with a female co-worker than he anticipates. There are many risks associated with this situation, particularly if the woman reports to him. In addition to the standard risks is the possibility of this kind of relationship leading to a charge of "sexual harassment." Having done training in corporations on Preventing Sexual Harassment, I know that any ambiguity about a male-female relationship on the job is a recipe for potential trouble.

So a close working relationship that crosses the line can be extremely dangerous—both in risk to professional reputation and to family stability. Since home and work are not as separate as is sometimes assumed, there's a realistic concern about potential harm to the wife if *any* kind of trouble develops from this situation.

The bottom line is that it's important to take definitive action to change the nature of any building sexual tension at work. Otherwise, the situation will only escalate over time. It's unwise, both personally and professionally, to sit back and hope it will resolve itself—since without intervention, it will almost certainly get even more complicated.

As to the nature of the actions to take, that depends on the specific situation and the people involved. But the first step is to do something to change the overall environment. This means going beyond simply deciding to "cool off" the personal relationship between the two people. Old habits of relating are hard to change unless the environment in which they take place changes.

So it means seeking ways to create more actual distance in the working relationship—either through one of the parties seeking a transfer to a different area of the company or other actions that preclude the kind of access they've had to each other up to that point.

Women

In the past (when there were fewer women in the workforce) most affairs at work involved married men and single women. But today the women are just as likely to be married as well. Since more women are having affairs in all areas of life than in the past, the workplace is no exception.

Today, there are more women in the workforce than ever before, and professionals spend an average of 52.5 hours a week on the job. The new working situation means that women often spend more time with their co-workers than with their friends or family.

Of course, it's not just the sheer amount of time that women spend at work; they also spend their work time in different ways. More and more women are traveling in conjunction with their jobs. This additional opportunity for close relationships to develop outside the normal work environment simply expands the opportunities to build close relationships with men at work.

Since women are more likely to associate feelings of closeness with sexual feelings, these friendships provide fertile ground for eventually becoming sexual relationships and developing into workplace affairs.

Part of the problem is that women often have a false perception of men at work as being more thoughtful and communicative than their husbands. However, these men are not particularly special in their ability to relate to women in a satisfying way. It's the circumstances that make the difference.

For instance, a man who seems so thoughtful and communicative at work may behave very differently at home. His wife sees a different side of him and may complain about him in much the same way as the woman he's having an affair with complains about her own husband.

While women have made great strides in achieving higher levels of employment, more often than not, it's still a man who is "the boss." Unfortunately, it's not uncommon for a woman to become infatuated with her boss, primarily due to his powerful position in her work life. Women often have a great deal of admiration for a boss's ability and success, and they may come to value him not only as a boss, but also as a friend and mentor. This kind of close working relationship can be extremely dangerous—with a strong likelihood of damaging her professional reputation.

In addition, the boss often has a lot of control over a woman's future in terms of her economic well-being and her opportunities for advancement. This is not to say that women are trying to "sleep their way to the top." Most ambitious women today clearly recognize that this is not a wise path to success. But the boss may play such an important part in a woman's life that she has difficulty separating their professional relationship from her personal feelings.

While both married men and married women are risking significant consequences both at home and at work, women's job-related risks are somewhat greater. When one of the people involved in an affair loses their job, it's almost certainly going to be the woman. The man is more likely to hold a higher position in the company and thus be more highly valued as an employee. So a woman having an affair at work is in double jeopardy in that she is more vulnerable to losing her job *and* her marriage.

Even if she's able to keep her job, her peers' assessment of her as a worker will probably be lowered. The double standard for judging sexual behavior that exists in society as a whole exists in the workplace as well. Both men and women are likely to be more harsh in their judgment of the woman than the man when it comes to a workplace affair. Even if co-workers bring no moral judgment to her actions, they're likely to make a professional judgment that she's not really serious about her career.

Another problem for co-workers is that workplace affairs often create situations that affect them personally. Some of the possible impacts include: having to "cover" for an affair, the amount of time an affair might take from a focus on business, special treatment or privileges that might accompany an affair, unfair distribution of labor by virtue of time spent on an affair, or just being distracted by the fact that an affair is taking place at work.

There's also the risk, of course, that a woman involved in an affair will be distracted by it herself. While most men have learned to compartmentalize their lives and separate their feelings from their ability to focus on other things, women may experience some difficulty in blocking out the dynamics of a workplace affair while trying to concentrate on their work.

With so much at stake, why does a woman take the risk of having a workplace affair? Part of the explanation is simply that she ignores or denies the risks. When caught up in the emotional high of the relationship, she focuses only on the pleasure and excitement involved, not on the potential consequences.

Having a workplace affair is not a smart decision for a woman, but most women never actually make that decision; they simply fall into an affair. Avoiding an affair at work requires deliberately deciding in advance not to get involved and continually reinforcing that decision by focusing on the risks.

The Role of "Management" in Preventing Affairs at Work

Very few companies deal directly with the issue of workplace affairs. If at all possible, they ignore this issue. In small companies, where it may be more difficult to ignore, there's more likelihood of action—but it's usually based on reacting to a given situation, not on having a clear policy. In most instances, it's simply not on the company's agenda as an issue to be dealt with.

One reason companies tend to avoid this issue is that monitoring people's personal lives is not generally seen as the responsibility of business unless it clearly interferes with productivity. So any effort the company makes toward curtailing sexual activity is usually in response to a specific demand from one or more individuals within the organization. And most of these demands take the form of complaints about sexual harassment rather than about affairs between two consenting employees.

Basically, the company only addresses whatever sexual problems it's *forced* to deal with. It's only when other employees officially complain and demand that something be done that the company is likely to take action.

Perhaps the most subtle, but most pervasive, reason companies don't take action in dealing with workplace affairs is that there's no separate entity called "The Company"; there are only individuals (usually men) in positions of authority. And many of these men are either involved in affairs themselves or are close personal friends with other men who are involved. Either way, they're less than eager to rock the boat.

Clearly, this is a sensitive issue that most people in business prefer to avoid. Since they feel there's no way they can win in dealing with it, they simply do nothing.

Survey Results for "Maintaining professional boundaries with co-workers"

Ranked #3 out of the 16 items on the list

52.2 percent of total respondents chose this among their top 5 items

All percentages below reflect how many respondents chose this among their top 5 items.

Women demonstrate a greater awareness of and concern about the risk of affairs in the workplace than do men.

56 percent of women

41 percent of men

The difference between those with personal experience and those with no experience is reflected in all comparisons below—which is typical of the responses to most of the items on the survey.

55 percent of all respondents with experience

44 percent of all respondents with no experience

58 percent of married women with experience

48 percent of married women with no experience

45 percent of married men with experience

36 percent of married men with no experience

Comments about Results for "Work"

Affairs that begin at work are extremely common, so it's not surprising that this item ranked #3 out of the 16 items. It's also not surprising that more women than men saw it as significant (56 percent to 41 percent). That's probably due to the fact that virtually all men work while many, but not all, women work. So there are more wives with working husbands than men with working wives. Therefore, wives (women) see this as a bigger area of concern.

The Bottom Line about "Work"

An awareness of the prevalence of workplace affairs should not be construed as saying they're inevitable. Quite the contrary. In fact, awareness of the potential can help prevent unintended liaisons from developing in the first place. This means being vigilant in monitoring your own thoughts and actions related to co-workers of the opposite sex.

It's important to take definitive action to change the nature of any building sexual tension at work—in order to defuse any significant ramifications. It's unwise, both personally and professionally, to sit back and hope that it will resolve itself. Without intervention, it will almost certainly get even more complicated. As described by Shirley Glass in her book *NOT "Just Friends,"* it's important to recognize the "slippery slope" and avoid ever starting down this path.

One way to avoid letting this situation get out of hand is to act on some of the prevention factors discussed earlier: having ongoing honest communication with the spouse and discussing attractions and temptations.

It may also be helpful to talk with a professional or someone else who is a "friend of the marriage." There's something about discussing your thinking out loud that allows you to view it more realistically, leading you to be more accountable and responsible.

Finally, you're not really losing anything when you make the effort to avoid workplace affairs. In fact, it's a win-win (for your marriage *and* your job) when you maintain professional boundaries with co-workers.

Chapter 14

• • • • • •

Avoiding personal relationships on the Internet

The Internet is becoming the newest, strongest "pick-up" place around these days. And it's so easy to get caught up in it that many people don't know what hit them until it's too late.

Most people are not *seeking* sex when they go online and go into a chat room. However, a big part of the problem is that people don't realize how this may be the eventual result of seemingly innocent online interactions.

The person involved in online interactions may have no intention of letting it become inappropriate and may deny (even to themselves) that it's happening, even as it's getting out of hand. Regardless of what is believed or intended regarding online relationships, they have a way of taking on a life of their own that takes on more and more importance in the overall scheme of things. Unfortunately, seemingly innocent online relationships are damaging (or outright destroying) many, many marriages.

In some of my other writings, I have described the most typical progression of online affairs.

Below is an overview of this all-too-common scenario.

1. You spend more and more time online.

- Online interactions provide an "escape" from the realities of day-to-day living.
- The fantasy world online can make the real world seem dull and boring.
- The sheer numbers of people create unlimited potential for "newness."

2. You meet someone interesting online.

- You share confidences: hopes, fears, fantasies.
- The intense sharing brings you closer and closer together.
- You fantasize about being more than online friends.
- You become infatuated with your "friend" and want much more interaction.
- You feel like you're "in love."

3. Your spouse suspects/knows about your online friend.

- You deny or rationalize about your online activity.
- Your spouse becomes more and more suspicious and threatened.
- You ignore or deny the impact this is having on your spouse.
- Your spouse learns more and is devastated by the situation.
- You tell yourself that since there's no actual sex involved, it shouldn't matter.
- You grow closer to your online friend and more distant from your spouse.

4. You want to meet your online friend in person.

- You feel like "soulmates" or that you were "meant for each other."

- You consider "risking it all" to see your online friend.

- You either meet and engage in sex or don't and feel like "star-crossed lovers."

5. Your life has been changed in ways you never intended.

- Your online relationship ends—and your marriage may end as well.

Many people try to rationalize that online affairs are not really affairs—since they don't involve sex (at least not in the beginning). But they have the potential for being as devastating to the spouse as a sexual affair. That's because any kind of behavior with sexual overtones that is kept secret from the spouse *feels* like an affair to the spouse if/when they find out about it. And even if the spouse doesn't find out, keeping this kind of secret creates distance in the marriage and interferes with the degree of closeness in the relationship.

The safest way to ensure that online interactions don't damage the marriage is to make sure that no online interactions are secret. This means not saying anything to someone online that you aren't willing for your spouse to read. Whenever someone invokes privacy rights, it's probably because they have something to hide. And hiding online relationships is not privacy; it's secrecy. Also, even if there's nothing serious happening at the moment, continuing to keep these interactions secret just increases the chances that they will eventually escalate as described above.

Infatuations with online relationships can become addictive; and the longer it goes on, the stronger the habit is likely to become. So even though it may be difficult to confront this issue, the situation is likely to get worse and become even more difficult to address after more time has passed.

Of course, even when you're committed to confronting this issue, it can be difficult to do it in an effective way—a way that moves the process forward rather than creating a win-lose competitive dynamic. Since there are so many ways to keep online activity secret, it's not enough to make a demand or issue an ultimatum. It's critical to get agreement (a "buy-in") on the part of the one involved on the Internet that they will change their habits.

Habits of *any* kind (like unhealthy eating habits, for instance) can be difficult to change, so the first step to actually making a change is that the person changing needs to *want* to make the change. It's not enough for others to want it on their behalf—or to try to force them to change. This means getting an agreement to be accountable in some measurable way.

For instance, people are much more likely to be responsible if they regularly "report" their progress. Again, as with weight loss or alcoholism, etc., group support (where others know how you're doing) can be an important factor in being successful. When people can ignore or hide their actions, it's much more difficult for them to change habitual behavior. But if they're placed in a position where they verbally report on their progress, it means they have to *lie* to avoid accountability.

Therefore, the first step is to establish a means of accountability. This involves identifying and agreeing on who will be the recipient of regular reports. Ideally, this would be the spouse, but if that's not workable for some reason, the next best choice would be a professional.

Also, reports would need to go beyond a simple statement of, "Yes, I did" or "No, I didn't." They would involve acknowledging frequency of thinking about it or being tempted—as well, of course, as any actual instances involving personal relationships on the Internet. And if there is *any* activity, it would need to be reported in detail as to when, where, with whom, for how long, etc.

Naturally, it's best to avoid ever beginning this pattern of making personal connections on the Internet. But this involves a great deal more education of the general public about the temptations and pitfalls of ever starting down this path. As each new person gains Internet access, they're often quite naïve about the risks (dangers) of getting carried along with the growing tide of personal connections to be found there. The scenario I described above can serve as a warning for those who don't understand how this happens—in order to avoid it.

Survey Results for "Avoiding personal relationships on the Internet"

Ranked #12 out of the 16 items on the list

19.1 percent of total respondents chose this among their top 5 items

All percentages below reflect how many respondents chose this among their top 5 items.

There was a striking difference in the responses of men vs. women—with this item being chosen by more women than men in all categories.

21 percent of women
12 percent of men

22 percent of married women with experience
14 percent of married men with experience

20 percent of married women with no experience
10 percent of married men with no experience

Comments about Results for "Internet"

Concerns about the Internet were remarkably low, considering the growing number of affairs that begin online. I suspect this low ranking (#12 out of 16) is only because many of the other items were more universally applicable, whereas this is a very specific area of concern.

One reason for the greater concern among women may be based on the number of men who visit porn sites on the Internet. While both women and men may become involved through chat rooms or other Internet outlets, men are far more likely to also frequent porn sites.

While men may not consider viewing porn to be relevant to affairs, wives may see this as a threat to the relationship, particularly since it is so often done in secrecy. And the working definition of an affair is any outside activity of a sexual or emotionally intimate nature that is engaged in secretly.

The Bottom Line about the "Internet"

Online affairs are a growing problem that is sure to get much bigger as more and more people come online. So everyone would be well-advised to be better informed about this newest dimension to extramarital affairs.

When most people first get Internet access, they are quite naïve about the risks of getting carried along with the growing tide of personal connections to be found there. The scenario I described earlier can serve as a guide for avoiding this all-too-common pitfall.

While an online affair begins without any physical contact, far more online activity moves over to the "real world" than people anticipate. In fact, according to the responses to a survey I conducted of people who had been involved in an online affair, almost half of them (49 percent) reported that they eventually had a physical sexual relationship.

So an online "friendship" is usually just the first step in an interaction that almost inevitably leads to *more*. Most people kid themselves that it won't get out of hand and that it's harmless. After it does get out of hand and develops beyond what was originally intended, it's often too late.

There's a fairly predictable pattern to online relationships. Understanding the progressive nature of these relationships provides an opportunity to stop the natural progression and avoid greater difficulties later.

The safest way to see that online interactions don't damage the primary relationship is to make sure that no online interactions are kept secret. This means getting your spouse to agree that neither of you will say anything to someone online that you aren't willing for the other one to read. And if anyone resists and invokes their right to privacy, it's probably because they already have something to hide. Then it's reasonable to be concerned— and to openly discuss those concerns rather than waiting until the situation inevitably escalates.

Chapter 15

• • • • • •

The bottom line

- The first step in preventing affairs is to recognize that although most people *intend* to be monogamous—no one is immune. With this awareness, you're better prepared to take the steps as an individual and as a couple that can help you prevent an affair in your marriage.

- Monogamy is not achieved through a one-time decision or condition that settles things once and for all. It's a challenge that must be met on a daily basis, with awareness and commitment. Preventing affairs is an ongoing process throughout the life of a long-term marriage.

- Preventing affairs requires letting go of the idea that you can rely *only* on your attitudes and beliefs to keep you safe. This means that you also need to demonstrate the kinds of ongoing actions and behaviors that will sustain your intention to be monogamous.

- You can't avoid affairs by *assuming* your marriage will be monogamous. My concern about this and other false assumptions about monogamy led to the title of my book *The Monogamy Myth*. (The "myth" refers to the "set of false assumptions" that people make about affairs, leaving them even more vulnerable.)

- The best way to avoid affairs on an ongoing basis is to fully commit to responsible honesty and to practice it throughout the marriage. Start talking now. Start from day one of the marriage. In fact, start long before you get married; start when you first begin getting serious.

- Don't pretend that neither of you will ever find anyone else attractive. Engage in ongoing honest communication about the reality of attractions and how to avoid the consequences of acting on them. The process of discussing attractions actually decreases the likelihood of acting on them because it focuses on the potential problems and consequences. And the effect on the relationship is to create a sense of closeness and a knowledge of each other that replaces suspicion with trust, making it more likely that your marriage will be monogamous.

- Don't let attractions develop into temptations through secrecy that serves to fuel the fantasy of acting on them. When a person is tempted to have an affair, their private thoughts usually dwell only on the potential pleasures. There's an added fascination and excitement about feelings that are kept secret as compared to those that are acknowledged and discussed. Shedding the cold light of day on secret desires goes a long way toward diminishing their power.

- **Honesty is the most important factor.** Although preventing affairs requires paying attention to *all* the potential factors that can lead someone to be tempted, honesty (or a lack thereof) is the "trump card" in determining whether or not someone acts on the temptation.

- Regardless of any reasons why a person may *want* to have an affair, they won't act on that desire unless they're willing to be dishonest and deceptive. Just as a lack of honesty is the strongest factor in *having* affairs, a commitment to honesty is the strongest factor in *preventing* affairs.

- There is no absolute protection from affairs. You have to fight for your marriage. You have to fight for honesty, and it's not an easy path.

- Recognize that the challenge is even greater because (despite giving lip service to monogamy), there are strong and pervasive factors in society that make it difficult to maintain monogamy. (See the Epilogue for a discussion of the "role of society" in preventing affairs.)

- As detailed in Chapter 11, there is no *one* reason why someone has an affair; affairs are the result of a combination of three broad *sets* of factors.
  o Factors that "push" people into affairs (problems, faults, shortcomings, etc.)
  o Factors that "pull" people into affairs (excitement, novelty, curiosity, etc.)
  o Societal factors (fascination/glamorization of affairs, selling of sex, lack of parent-child discussions of sex, secrecy)

The "push" factors and the "pull" factors are within the realm of responsibility of the individual and the couple. The "societal factors" are the responsibility of all of us.

- Parents play a particularly critical role in preventing affairs—because the road toward affairs begins long before marriage; in fact, long before *any* sexual activity. It

103

begins with the inability to talk realistically and honestly about sex and sexual issues. The lack of open communication between parents and children establishes a mindset that "sex and secrecy" go hand in hand. By the time a child grows up, they've been well-conditioned to be deceptive about their sexual thoughts and actions. This pattern continues into marriage, making it difficult to establish the kind of responsible honesty that's so essential to preventing affairs. (See the Epilogue for a discussion of the "role of parents.")

• Once you're an adult, you still have the opportunity to overcome the "conditioning in deception" that occurred while hiding your sexual activities from your parents. While it's more difficult to start being open and honest about sexual issues after years of being deceptive as a teenager, it *can* be done. Like a saying in T.A. (Transactional Analysis): *"What you are may be your parents' fault. But if you stay that way, it's your own fault."*

The Future of Monogamy

There are those who see a bleak outlook for the prospects of long-term monogamy in the future. In fact, I read one strange, sad comment that said: *"It's possible that there will be more monogamy in the future (even without better educating the public about the reality of affairs)—only due to the fact that marriages are lasting a shorter and shorter time period and people may be better able to maintain monogamy for those shorter periods."*

Long-term monogamy *can* be achieved by any couple who acknowledge they're not immune and deliberately work together to make it happen. This involves changing a lot of old ways of thinking and relating, and it involves committing to "responsible honesty" on an ongoing basis.

Since sustaining monogamy requires a comprehensive effort (not leaving it to each individual couple), there needs to be much more genuine support from society at large. As a society, we all need to acknowledge our role in perpetuating affairs and take more responsibility for dealing with the societal factors that support affairs.

The bottom line is that *everyone* has a role to play in preventing affairs.

Epilogue:

The Special Roles of Society and of Parents

This section focuses on the larger context within which affairs take place, with emphasis on the role of society as a whole, showing the many ways all of us can support couples in successfully preventing affairs.

It also points out the special role of parents in preventing affairs for future generations.

Role of Society (All of Us) in Preventing Affairs

Since the prevalence of affairs and the pain caused by affairs affects everyone in some way, it's time to think more seriously about the role we all play in society's adolescent way of dealing with affairs. Affairs are often seen only as entertainment or fodder for gossip—until it happens to you! When it becomes real, it's a very different matter. And if it doesn't happen to you, it will certainly happen to someone close to you. So affairs are everybody's business. No one is exempt from being affected by affairs—or from their responsibility for contributing to affairs.

Here are some of the ways we contribute to affairs:

—*On an individual basis throughout society:* The traditional approach (unless it touches us personally) is to deal with this issue by simply ignoring it, denying it, or condemning it. Unfortunately, this does nothing either to help deter affairs or to deal with their consequences.

—*On a couple basis*: The primary way most couples approach monogamy is to *assume* it when they marry and take the vows. They fail to take the kinds of actions throughout the marriage to sustain their commitment to monogamy.

—*On a societal basis:* We give a lot of lip service to monogamy, but do virtually nothing positive to reinforce monogamy. In fact, we undermine it at every turn. We say affairs are horrible, but inadvertently support affairs through our participation in the many societal factors that contribute to affairs.

The Societal Factors

There's a general belief that society as a whole is supportive of monogamy, leading people to believe that if an affair happens to them, it's due *only* to personal failure. This kind of thinking leads to feelings of personal blame, personal shame, and almost universal devastation.

However, affairs are due to more than *just* personal failure; personal actions take place within the larger context of the society as a whole. So while we as a society claim to support monogamy, we actually contribute to some significant societal factors that support and encourage affairs.

This is not to say that all the blame should be placed on society. But if we're to understand and more effectively deal with this issue, it's essential that we look at the societal context within which affairs take place.

Here are some of the societal factors mentioned earlier, which are discussed more thoroughly in *The Monogamy Myth:*

- the overall fascination with affairs (and the titillation involved)
- the glorification of affairs in movies, TV, romance novels, music
- our sex-saturated culture that uses sex to sell almost everything
- a "code of secrecy" that protects those having affairs from dealing with the consequences
- the lack of honest discussions about sex by parents with their children.

(Note: I've devoted the entire following chapter to focusing on the last factor listed above: the lack of honest discussions of sex by parents when raising their children.)

Through the years as I worked on developing ways for people to better understand and deal with extramarital affairs, I came to see that the dishonesty about affairs is part of a much larger issue—the general dishonesty about sex in our society as a whole.

Frankly, it's tough to sustain an honest marriage within a dishonest society. It's like swimming upstream against a very strong current. It takes a tremendous effort to make any headway at all. On the other hand, swimming downstream is a cinch. It takes very little effort to simply go along for the ride.

This is what happens all too often. We take what we think is the easy way out, just keeping our thoughts to ourselves. It's no wonder we often give up on our relationships when the level of withheld thoughts and feelings seems too great to overcome.

Frankly, as a society we're "sick" when it comes to affairs. In fact, we're positively schizophrenic. We condemn affairs on

108

the one hand—while at the same time relishing every fascinating tidbit of the latest scandal or piece of gossip around the office, in the neighborhood, or in the media. While we condemn any "real person" who has an affair, we devour all the movies about affairs, often rooting for the person who is having an affair (especially when it's a story like in *Bridges of Madison County*).

Again, my thinking about the impact of society has more recently been reflected in Esther Perel's book *Mating in Captivity*: *"We live in a world that offers us little help with staying put or making do. Nowhere are we encouraged to be satisfied with what we have...We are convinced that sexual gratification and personal happiness go hand in hand. No wonder people often feel restless in marriage."*

As a society, we need to acknowledge our role in perpetuating affairs and take more responsibility for dealing with the societal factors that support affairs. We also need to adopt a more compassionate attitude toward the people whose lives are affected by affairs. It's hard enough on those personally dealing with this issue without compounding their pain by our harsh way of judging them.

This change in attitude is particularly appropriate in view of the fact that people don't have affairs in isolation; they have them within the context of a society (made up of all of us) that actually contributes to the difficulty in preventing affairs.

It's my hope that more understanding and perspective can bring support to those individuals who face it personally and bring change to us as a society of people who care about making things better, both for today and for future generations.

Role of Parents in Prevention for Future Generations

What about future generations? How can we help them be better equipped to prevent affairs in their own marriages when they become adults?

The first step is to recognize that the patterns of dishonesty and deception that are inherent in affairs get established very early in life—as teenagers hiding our sex lives from our parents. We bring this experience with deception into our marriages and use it in hiding our affairs from our spouse.

So regardless of what steps a couple may take to prevent affairs, they're fighting an uphill battle if they were raised in the typical way—where parents fail to talk openly and honestly with them about sex when they are growing up.

For generations, we have not been prepared to deal honestly with sexual issues. Our parents are seldom honest with us about sex when we're young. Very few children get good, clear facts about sex, and almost none of us get sound information about sexuality and sexual love. In fact, we're actually conditioned to be dishonest about sex when we're growing up. We're all well-trained in deception and dishonesty about sex, starting when we're born and continuing throughout our childhood and teenage years.

As teenagers we're unable to talk honestly with our parents about sex, so we present a false image to our parents when we become sexually active. We need to take a hard look at the price we pay for this dishonesty. It's far too high, both as children struggling to deal with our fears and questions—and as adults struggling to develop trust and intimacy.

Some Facts about Teenage Sexual Activity

- According to a study published in 2007 by *Public Health Reports,* the journal of the U.S. Public Health Service, 75 percent of U.S. teens have premarital sex by age 20, and 58 percent have it before age 18.

- According to a 2006 report by the Centers for Disease Control and Prevention, students are increasingly likely to be sexually active as they move through adolescence.

  This report indicates the following percentages have had intercourse:

	Boys	Girls
Before age 13	9%	4%
9th grade	39%	29%
10th grade	42%	44%
11th grade	51%	52%
12th grade	64%	62%

(Note: In their 2005 report, about 14 percent of teenagers reported having sexual intercourse with four or more people during their high school years.)

- In 2007, a national study commissioned by Congress revealed that abstinence education has little to no effect on the sexual practices of teenagers.

The Responsibility of Parents

A lot of the responsibility for preventing affairs for future generations depends on our actions as parents when raising our children. We need to establish a strong line of parent-child communication about sexual issues in order to establish a pattern of honesty about sex.

Unfortunately, this seldom happens, so most children feel they can't talk to their parents about sex and develop a habit of deception when they become teenagers, presenting a false image to their parents. When a teenager is dating and knows they're *supposed* to avoid sexual activity (but they want to do it), they usually wind up doing it in a secretive way, while pretending to their parents that they're not.

The same pattern continues in adulthood. By the time we get married we've had plenty of practice at being deceptive and dishonest about sex. So when a married person is tempted to have an affair, they often go ahead and do it in a secretive way, while pretending to their spouse that they're not.

For instance, when I found out about the numerous affairs my husband had over a 7-year period early in our marriage, I kept thinking, *"How could he have done such a thing?"* I was overwhelmed by the contrast with his image of being a faithful husband during that time. He seemed almost like a stranger as I became aware of this new information. It seemed impossible that he could have been so deceptive. After realizing this was the kind of pretense he'd learned when we were teenagers hiding our sex lives from our parents, I could better understand how he did it.

I also realized that just as our parents didn't question us directly about their suspicions when we were teenagers, I didn't question him directly about my suspicions of his affairs. At all stages of our lives the primary way we deal with sexual issues

is to close our eyes and hope for the best. This kind of coopera-
tion in the deception is an important factor in understanding
how it happens.

What Can Parents Do?

The first task for parents is to establish good lines of
communication regarding sexual issues of all kinds, with an
emphasis on the importance of honesty. Frankly, we won't have
much impact on the prevalence of affairs until that happens.

I first addressed the important role of parents in *The
Monogamy Myth*.

We can make a significant difference in the prevention of
affairs if we begin raising kids who don't learn that "sex and
secrecy" go hand in hand. This means being more willing to
realistically face the sexual realities of teenagers today by
making it possible for them to talk to us about sexual issues.

This need will grow ever more critical with the expanding
influence of the Internet—which will expose future generations
to more explicit sexually oriented material than TV or movies
ever did. They will use the Internet as we currently use the
telephone, and no efforts at censorship or "protection" can
address the problems they will face as a result.

Our hope for influencing their development into sexually
responsible adults lies in our commitment to more honest
communication about all aspects of sex, monogamy, relationships, and marriage. Of course, this means "practicing what we
preach" by demonstrating within the family the importance of
honest communication. Future generations can only learn
honesty by seeing it in their own families.

So by helping our own relationships become more
honest, we provide the kind of training that makes it more
likely that our children will have relationships based on a

commitment to honesty. This increase in the level of honesty between couples can greatly enhance the satisfaction that's possible in a loving relationship, as well as reducing the likelihood of extramarital affairs.

Your Greatest Challenge

"Eighty percent of parents agree that it is their responsibility to talk with their kids about sex, yet few actually do so."

This statement is the conclusion of a coalition of organizations attending a one-day colloquium on this issue, including the American Medical Association, the American School Health Association, the Association of Junior Leagues, the Girls Clubs of America, the Alan Guttmacher Institute, and New York University.

When young people go through their teen years being dishonest and deceptive with their parents about sex, they're likely to continue that pattern as adults in being dishonest with their spouses as they engage in affairs.

Keeping open the lines of communication is the real challenge you face as a parent today. Forget about control; that's a false idea anyway, since you do not have ultimate control over their actions. But you do have the ability to *influence* your teen—if you avoid making this a power struggle.

This does not mean that you are settling for less; quite the contrary. It means you're pursuing a more significant goal (being able to influence your teen) that will allow you to have a much greater impact on your teen's well-being.

Some Ideas to Help You Face this Challenge

- Acknowledge that your teenager is probably going to experiment with sex. Help them do so honestly and responsibly. Forget about "Just say no." It doesn't work; never has and never will.

- Encourage your teenager to come to you with any and all questions, fears, or concerns; and when they do, never discount them—no matter what they have to say.

- Put your critical/judgmental side behind lock and key, even though this will take some work.

- Build trust by sharing, when they are relevant, your own thoughts, feelings, and experiences when you were their age. Resist the temptation to use platitudes or to lecture.

- Avoid focusing your comments about sex only on "negatives." It's important to *also* reinforce the gentle, caring, pleasurable aspects of loving sex.

Demonstrating Honesty

As the parent of a teen, you may have said, *"You can come to me with any questions,"* or *"You can talk to me about anything."* But most teens won't feel safe to do that unless you go first by showing it's a two-way street. Only if they hear that you had some of the same questions and concerns when you were a teenager are they likely to believe you actually understand what they're going through.

So if you want your kids to come to you with their problems and concerns about sexual matters (and other problems as well), you might better achieve this by setting an example, by telling your kids about your own time as a teenager and how you felt and acted regarding sexual matters.

You may be very uncomfortable with this whole idea of being honest with your kids about sex. Understandably, you might prefer to forget (or hide) some of your own teenage experiences, but telling them is not as much a risk as you might think because they see through the hypocrisy anyway.

It may help to remind yourself that it's not a matter of "show and tell." In fact, the main teaching is not about sex per se, it's about the importance of honesty—honesty in *all* important matters. You're educating your teens about much more than sex. You're helping them grow in their ability to make good choices and to decide important issues in life for themselves.

Breaking the Cycle

You may feel so overwhelmed by the whole issue of teenage sexuality that you'd prefer to ignore it altogether. But if you do, you'll only perpetuate the failure that's been passed down for generations in not helping young people deal with their sexuality in a healthy, responsible way.

Here's what you can do to break the cycle of dishonesty and deception between parents and teens:

- Give your teen good, factual information.
- Acknowledge their desires, fears, motivations, and pressures.
- Be honest with your teen by sharing relevant information about your own teen years.
- Discuss with them their alternatives instead of laying out absolute demands.
- Guide them in making informed choices.
- Support them in their effort to be responsible.
- "Be there" for them—no matter what.

116

The bottom line is that the primary responsibility for preventing affairs in future generations rests with us as parents.

Appendix I

Questionnaire and Overview of Responses
Survey Questionnaire on Preventing Affairs

While there may be no absolute guarantees for affair-proofing a marriage, it's wise to try to identify which factors may make affairs much less likely. To participate in this survey, please respond to the following questions:

Gender:
 male
 female

Marital Experience:
 never married
 currently married or previously married

Have you had personal experience in dealing with an affair?
 no—Neither I nor my partner has had an affair
 yes—I have had personal experience (see clarification below)
 Check "yes" if:
 —you are (or were) married and either you or your partner had an affair
 —you are (or were) in a committed relationship and one of you had an affair
 —you are single and had an affair with a married person

Check the 5 items you think are most likely to prevent affairs:
 Marrying someone with similar background and values
 Taking the marriage vows seriously/intending to be faithful
 Being in love with your partner
 Having mutual trust
 Having high moral principles and/or religious convictions
 Having ongoing honest communication about all issues
 Maintaining professional boundaries with co-workers
 Acknowledging and discussing attractions to others
 Avoiding personal relationships on the Internet
 Having a satisfying marital sex life
 Trying to meet your partner's needs
 Repeating/renewing the marriage vows
 Having children together and being a devoted mother/father
 Being concerned about hurting your partner and the children
 Being afraid of getting caught, risking possible divorce
 Having no opportunity - no free time, never travel, etc.
 Other (please specify)

Overview of Responses

Total Respondents: 755

Gender
    Female—575
    Male—180

Marital Status
    Married—728
    Single—27

Personal Experience
    Yes—552
    No—203

Combinations of Responses:
    Female-Married: Yes—435
    Female-Married: No—116
    Male-Married: Yes—104
    Male-Married: No—73
    Female-Single: Yes—11
    Female-Single: No—13

All Respondents: 755

Items	Responses	%	Rank
honesty	599	79.3%	1
vows	397	52.6%	2
work	394	52.2%	3
morals	316	41.9%	4
needs	274	36.3%	5
sex	268	35.5%	6
trust	263	34.8%	7
attractions	258	34.2%	8
hurt	244	32.3%	9
similarities	187	24.8%	10
love	185	24.5%	11
Internet	144	19.1%	12
fear	55	7.3%	13
children	50	6.6%	14
opportunity	41	5.4%	15
recommitment	25	3.0%	16
Other	171		

Female: 575

Items	Total	%	Rank
honesty	470	82%	1
work	320	56%	2
vows	293	51%	3
morals	220	38%	4
attractions	217	38%	5
trust	205	36%	6
hurt	194	34%	7
needs	192	33%	8
sex	181	31%	9
similarities	143	25%	10
love	130	23%	11
Internet	122	21%	12
opportunity	40	7%	13
fear	37	6%	14
children	27	5%	15
recommitment	19	3%	16
Other	124		

Male: 180

Items	Total	%	Rank
honesty	129	72%	1
vows	104	58%	2
morals	96	53%	3
sex	87	48%	4
needs	82	46%	5
work	74	41%	6
trust	58	32%	7
love	55	31%	8
hurt	50	28%	9
similarities	44	24%	10
attractions	41	23%	11
children	23	13%	12
Internet	22	12%	13
fear	18	10%	14
recommitment	6	3%	15
opportunity	1	1%	16
Other	47		

Overview of Responses

Married: 728

Items	Total	%	Rank
honesty	580	80%	1
vows	385	53%	2
work	382	52%	3
morals	306	42%	4
needs	265	36%	5
trust	254	35%	6 tie
sex	254	35%	6 tie
attractions	251	34%	8
hurt	235	32%	9
similarities	175	24%	10 tie
love	175	24%	10 tie
Internet	140	19%	12
fear	53	7%	13
children	47	6%	14
opportunity	38	5%	15
recommitment	21	3%	16
Other	165		

Single: 27

Items	Total	%	Rank
honesty	19	70%	1
sex	14	52%	2
similarities	12	44%	3 tie
vows	12	44%	3 tie
work	12	44%	3 tie
love	10	37%	6 tie
morals	10	37%	6 tie
trust	9	33%	8 tie
needs	9	33%	8 tie
hurt	9	33%	8 tie
attractions	7	26%	11
Internet	4	15%	12
recommitment	4	15%	13
children	3	11%	14
opportunity	3	11%	15
fear	2	7%	16
Other	6		

Yes (with personal experience): 552

Items	Total	%	Rank
honesty	471	85%	1
work	305	55%	2
vows	269	49%	3
attractions	224	41%	4
needs	200	36%	5
morals	188	34%	6 tie
sex	188	34%	6 tie
hurt	184	33%	8
trust	179	32%	9
love	131	24%	10
similarities	121	22%	11
Internet	112	20%	12
fear	42	8%	13
opportunity	37	7%	14
children	28	5%	15
recommitment	20	4%	16
Other	125		

No (without personal experience): 203

Items	Total	%	Rank
vows	128	63%	1 tie
morals	128	63%	1 tie
honesty	128	63%	1 tie
work	89	44%	4
trust	84	41%	5
sex	80	39%	6
needs	74	36%	7
similarities	66	33%	8
hurt	60	30%	9
love	54	27%	10
attractions	34	17%	11
Internet	32	16%	12
children	22	11%	13
fear	13	6%	14
recommitment	5	2%	15
opportunity	4	2%	16
Other	46		

Female-Married: Yes—435

Items	Total	%	Rank
honesty	378	87%	1
work	253	58%	2
vows	210	48%	3
attractions	190	44%	4
hurt	150	34%	5
needs	145	33%	6
trust	144	33%	7
morals	140	32%	8
sex	125	29%	9
Internet	95	22%	10
similarities	90	21%	11 tie
love	90	21%	11 tie
opportunity	35	8%	13 tie
fear	31	7%	13 tie
children	17	4%	15
recommitment	13	3%	16
Other	93		

Female-Married: No—116

Items	Total	%	Rank
honesty	75	65%	1
vows	74	64%	2
morals	72	62%	3
work	56	48%	4
trust	52	45%	5
sex	45	39%	6
similarities	43	37%	7
needs	38	33%	8
hurt	36	31%	9
love	30	26%	10
Internet	23	20%	11
attractions	20	17%	12
children	8	7%	13
fear	4	3%	14
recommitment	2	2%	15
opportunity	2	2%	16
Other	13		

Male-Married: Yes—104

Items	Total	%	Rank
honesty	83	80%	1
sex	53	51%	2
vows	52	50%	3
needs	50	48%	4
work	47	45%	5
morals	41	39%	6
love	35	34%	7
trust	30	29%	8 tie
attractions	30	29%	8 tie
hurt	29	28%	10
similarities	23	22%	11
Internet	15	14%	12
fear	13	13%	13
children	9	9%	14
recommitment	4	4%	15
opportunity	0	0%	16
Other	29		

Male-Married: No—73

Items	Total	%	Rank
morals	53	73%	1
vows	49	67%	2
honesty	44	60%	3
sex	32	44%	4 tie
needs	32	44%	4 tie
trust	28	38%	6
work	26	36%	7
love	20	27%	8 tie
hurt	20	27%	8 tie
similarities	19	26%	10
children	13	18%	11
attractions	11	15%	12
Internet	7	10%	13
fear	5	7%	14
recommitment	2	3%	15
opportunity	1	1%	16
Other	17		

Female-Single: Yes—11

Items	Total	%	Rank
honesty	9	82%	1
sex	8	73%	2
similarities	6	55%	3 tie
love	6	55%	3 tie
work	5	45%	5 tie
vows	5	45%	5 tie
trust	5	45%	5 tie
needs	5	45%	5 tie
morals	5	45%	5 tie
hurt	4	36%	10 tie
attractions	4	36%	10 tie
recommitment	3	27%	12
opportunity	2	18%	13
Internet	2	18%	14
fear	2	18%	15
children	1	9%	16
Other	3		

Female-Single: No—13

Items	Total	%	Rank
honesty	8	62%	1
work	6	46%	2
vows	4	31%	3 tie
similarities	4	31%	3 tie
trust	4	31%	3 tie
needs	4	31%	3 tie
love	4	31%	3 tie
hurt	4	31%	3 tie
sex	3	23%	9 tie
morals	3	23%	9 tie
attractions	3	23%	9 tie
Internet	2	15%	12
recommitment	1	8%	13
opportunity	1	8%	14
children	1	8%	15
fear	0	0%	16
Other	2		

Appendix II

Rankings of Responses to Questionnaire

Here is the way the items were ranked, based on the percentages of total respondents choosing any given item among their top 5.

1. honesty: 79.3% (having ongoing honest communication about all marital issues)
2. vows: 52.6% (taking the marriage vows seriously/intending to be faithful)
3. work: 52.2% (maintaining professional boundaries with co-workers)
4. morals: 41.9% (having high moral principles and/or strong religious convictions)
5. needs: 36.3% (trying to meet your partner's needs)
6. sex: 35.5% (having a satisfying marital sex life)
7. trust: 34.8% (having mutual trust)
8. attractions: 34.2% (acknowledging and discussing attractions to others)
9. hurt: 32.3% (being concerned about hurting your partner and the children)
10. similarities: 24.8% (marrying someone with similar background and values)
11. love: 24.5% (being in love with your partner)
12. Internet: 19.1% (avoiding personal relationships on the Internet)
13. fear: 7.3% (being afraid of getting caught, risking possible divorce)
14. children: 6.6% (having children together and being a devoted mother/father)
15. opportunity: 5.4% (having no opportunity—no free time, never travel, etc.)
16. recommitment: 3.0% (repeating/renewing the marriage vows)

It was enormously gratifying to see that "honesty" was chosen among the top 5 items by more respondents than any other factor, making it both the most important *perceived* prevention factor as well as the most important *actual* factor.

Breakdowns (by sub-groups) of those who responded:

575 were female and 180 were male

728 were married and 27 were single

552 had personal experience and 203 had no personal experience

Top 5 Rankings of Sub-groups

Breakdown between Females and Males

Female:

1. having ongoing honest communication about all marital issues
2. maintaining professional boundaries with co-workers
3. taking marriage vows seriously/intending to be monogamous
4. having high moral principles and/or strong religious convictions
5. acknowledging and discussing attractions to others

Male:

1. having ongoing honest communication about all marital issues
2. taking marriage vows seriously/intending to be monogamous
3. having high moral principles and/or strong religious convictions
4. having a satisfying marital sex life
5. trying to meet your partner's needs

Comparisons of Rankings of Females and Males

Female	Male
1. honesty	1. honesty
2. work	2. vows
3. vows	3. morals
4. morals	4. sex
5. attractions	5. needs
6. trust	6. work
7. hurt	7. trust
8. needs	8. love
9. sex	9. hurt

Most Striking Differences by Gender

Attractions

Females ranked it #5.

It didn't appear in the top 9 rankings among males.

Sex

Males ranked it #4.

Females ranked it #9.

Breakdown between Married and Single

Married

1. having ongoing honest communication about all marital issues
2. taking marriage vows seriously/intending to be monogamous
3. maintaining professional boundaries with co-workers
4. having high moral principles and/or strong religious convictions
5. trying to meet your partner's needs

Single

1. having ongoing honest communication about all marital issues
2. having a satisfying marital sex life
3. marrying someone with similar background and values
4. taking marriage vows seriously/intending to be monogamous
5. maintaining professional boundaries with co-workers

Comparisons of Rankings of Married and Single

Married	Single
1. honesty	1. honesty
2. vows	2. sex
3. work	3. similarities
4. morals	4. vows
5. needs	5. work
6. trust	6. love
7. sex	7. morals
8. attractions	8. trust
9. hurt	9. needs/hurt (tie)

Most Striking Differences by Marital Status

Sex

Singles ranked it #2.

Marrieds ranked it #6, tied with "trust."

Love

Singles ranked it #6.

It didn't appear in the top 9 rankings among marrieds.

Breakdown between those with Personal Experience and those with No Personal Experience

With Personal Experience:
1. having ongoing honest communication about all marital issues
2. maintaining professional boundaries with co-workers
3. taking marriage vows seriously/intending to be monogamous
4. acknowledging and discussing attractions to others
5. trying to meet your partner's needs

Without Personal Experience:
(Note: first 3 items were tied)
1. having ongoing honest communication about all marital issues
2. taking marriage vows seriously/intending to be monogamous
3. having high moral principles and/or strong religious convictions
4. maintaining professional boundaries with co-workers
5. having mutual trust

Comparisons of Rankings of those with Personal Experience and those without
(Note: first 3 items under "No" were tied)

Yes	No
1. honesty	1. honesty
2. work	2. vows
3. vows	3. morals
4. attractions	4. work
5. needs	5. trust
6. morals	6. sex
7. sex	7. needs
8. hurt	8. similarities
9. trust	9. hurt

Most Striking Differences by Experience

Attractions
Those with experience ranked it #4.
It didn't appear in the top 9 among those without experience.

Morals
Those without experience ranked it #3.
Those with personal experience ranked it #6.

Breakdown Based on Groupings
—female-married: personal experience
—female-married: no personal experience
—male-married: personal experience
—male-married: no personal experience
—female-single: personal experience
—female-single: no personal experience

Female-married:
personal experience
1. honesty
2. work
3. vows
4. attractions
5. hurt

Female-married:
no personal experience
1. honesty
2. vows
3. morals
4. work
5. trust

Male-married:
personal experience
1. honesty
2. sex
3. vows
4. needs
5. work

Male-married:
no personal experience
1. morals
2. vows
3. honesty
4. sex
5. needs
(Note: "sex" and "needs" are tied)

Female-single:
personal experience
1. honesty
2. sex
3. similarities
4. love
5. work
(Note: "similarities" and "love" are tied)

Female-single:
no personal experience
1. honesty
2. work
3. vows
4. similarities
5. trust
(Note: "vows, similarities, trust" are tied)

Bibliography

· · · · · · ·

None of these books are exclusively about *preventing* affairs, but some include sections on prevention, and all are excellent resources on marriage and affairs.

Alan, Richard. *First Aid for the Betrayed*. Victoria, B.C.: Trafford Publishing, 2006.

Bercht, Anne. *My Husband's Affair Became the Best Thing That Ever Happened to Me*. Victoria, B.C.: Trafford Publishing, 2004.

Brown, Emily. *Affairs*. San Francisco: Jossey-Bass, 1999.

Carder, Dave. *Close Calls*. Chicago: Northfield Publishing, 2008.

Carder, Dave. *Torn Asunder*. Chicago: Moody Publishers, 1995.

Fisher, Helen E. *Anatomy of Love: The Natural History of Monogamy, Adultery, and Divorce*. New York: Fawcett Book Group, 1994.

Fisher, Helen. *Why We Love: The Nature and Chemistry of Romantic Love*. New York: Henry Holt and Co., 2004.

Glass, Shirley. *NOT "Just Friends."* New York: Simon & Schuster, Inc., 2003.

Gottman, John H. and Silver, Nan. *The Seven Principles for Making Marriage Work*. New York: Crown Publishers, Inc., 1999.

Haltzman, Scott. *The Secrets of Happily Married Men.* San Francisco: Jossey-Bass, 2005.

Harley, Willard F. Jr. *Surviving an Affair.* Grand Rapids MI: Revell Books, 1998.

Lusterman, Don-David. *Infidelity: A Survival Guide.* Oakland, CA: New Harbinger Publications, 1998.

Maheu, Marlene M. and Subotnik, Rona. *Infidelity on the Internet.* Holbrook, MA: Bob Adams, 1994.

McCarthy, Barry and McCarthy, Emily J. *Getting it Right the First Time.* London, England: Brunner/Routledge, 2004.

Neuman, M. Gary. *Emotional Infidelity.* New York: Three Rivers Press, 2002.

Perel, Esther. *Mating in Captivity.* San Francisco: Harper Paperbacks, 2007.

Phillips, Adam. *Monogamy.* United Kingdom: Vintage Books, 1999.

Pittman, Frank. *Private Lies.* New York: W. W. Norton, 1990.

Snyder, Douglas K., Baucom, Donald H. and Gordon, Kristina Coop. *Getting Past the Affair.* New York: The Guilford Press, 2007.

Spring, Janis Abrahms. *After the Affair.* New York: HarperCollins, 1997.

Staheli, Lana. *Affair-Proof Your Marriage.* San Francisco: Harper Paperbacks, 1998.

Subotnik, Rona, and Harris, Gloria. *Surviving Infidelity.* Holbrook, MA: Bob Adams, 1994

Vaughan, James and Peggy. *Beyond Affairs.* La Jolla, CA: Dialog Press, 1980.

Vaughan, James and Peggy. *Making Love Stay.* New York: HarperCollins Publishers, 1994.

Vaughan, Peggy. *The Monogamy Myth.* New York: Newmarket Press, 1989, 1998, 2003.

Weiner-Davis, Michele. *Divorce Busting.* New York: Simon & Schuster, 1993.

Acknowledgments

• • • • • • •

I'm grateful to all the people who have shared their personal experiences in dealing with affairs over the past 30 years. It is through their stories that I came to see how much we've failed to understand what's involved in preventing affairs.

I am thankful to Dr. Barry McCarthy for his helpful feedback on an early draft of the book. As an expert on sexuality and author of many books, his support for this project is greatly appreciated.

I want to acknowledge a special debt of gratitude to Diane Sollee, Director, Coalition for Marriage, Family and Couples Education (SmartMarriages.com). In addition to her personal and professional support for all my work, I particularly appreciate her help in getting out the word about my survey questionnaire on preventing affairs. Sending a notice to her listserv allowed me to reach a larger and more diverse audience than would have been possible without her help.

I deeply appreciate the support of my longtime friend and literary agent, Laurie Harper, as well as my association with the wonderful people at Newmarket Press, Esther Margolis, Keith Hollaman, and Harry Burton.

I'm also grateful to my personal support system: James, my husband of more than 50 years, my son Andy, my daughter and son-in-law, Vicki and Dan, and my three wonderful grand-daughters.

About the Author

Peggy Vaughan is an internationally recognized expert in the area of extramarital affairs. Beginning in 1980 with the publication of her personal story in *Beyond Affairs*, Peggy was thrust into a position of responding to the many people across the country who identified with her experience and sought her help. She formed a national support group in the early eighties, and used what she learned from that experience to present a new understanding of affairs in *The Monogamy Myth*.

Peggy's "societal perspective" of affairs has catapulted her into the forefront of the growing public discussion of this issue, where she is called upon to comment on the constant stream of news stories related to affairs. But it's her personal commitment to helping people recover from the emotional impact of a partner's affair that has gained her a worldwide following.

The primary arena for her ongoing work with this issue is the Internet, where she maintains an extensive website (www.dearpeggy.com) containing free information about extramarital affairs. On the web since 1996, this site serves as an Extramarital Affairs Resource Center. Beyond the information on the site itself, she provides links to other resources, including to BAN (Beyond Affairs Network, the support group she founded) as well as to related sites about the issue of affairs. She also supports the work of others by listing reviews she has written of books about affairs by other authors, as well as an extensive list for Locating a Therapist who has been recommended as being effective in dealing with affairs.

Peggy has been married for fifty-five years, has two grown children and three grandchildren, and makes her home in San Diego, California.

In addition to *The Monogamy Myth*, Peggy has written *Beyond Affairs*, *Making Love Stay*, and *Life-Design Workbook*, all co-authored with her husband, James.

TO HAVE AND TO HOLD
A PERSONAL HANDBOOK FOR BUILDING A STRONG MARRIAGE AND PREVENTING AFFAIRS

Based on Peggy Vaughan's 30 years of work with married couples and the issues of affairs, this important book challenges the assumption that monogamy can be taken for granted, and provides the tools for building a strong marriage and preventing affairs.

"You can't afford not to read this book! This book is a concise, quick read that can prevent your marriage from unexpected disaster. Peggy has identified, and so accurately described, what doesn't work in affair prevention as well as what does work." —Anne Bercht, author of *My Husband's Affair Became the Best Thing That Ever Happened to Me*

"A gold mine of wisdom. This book is one that every married couple should read and it is never too late. Simply stated, anyone in a committed relationship who wants to preserve it must read this book!" —Richard Alan, author of *First Aid for the Betrayed*

"This incredible book teaches us the secrets needed to commit to a lifetime of honesty and respect, not just on our wedding day but for each day of a loving marriage. It is essential reading." —from a Reader

144 pages. 5½" x 8½". ISBN 978-1-55704-851-6. $14.95. Paperback. Also available as an ebook.

MONOGAMY MYTH
A PERSONAL HANDBOOK FOR RECOVERING FROM AFFAIRS

Acclaimed by readers, reviewers, and counselors, this is the best book to help couple understand why affairs happen and how to handle suspicion and confrontation, cope with pain, build self-esteem, and decide whether to go or to stay.

"An outstanding and wonderfully helpful book." —Harriet Lerner, Ph.D., author of *The Dance of Anger*

"In a personal voice Peggy Vaughan packs years of expertise into a compelling, down-to-earth guide for couples seeking to survive the trauma of extramarital affairs." —Janis Abrahms Spring, Ph.D., author of *After the Affair*

"This book saved my marriage, and probably my sanity—and maybe my very life." —from a Reader

256 pages. 5½" x 8½". ISBN 978-1-55704-542-3. $14.95. Paperback. Also available as an ebook.

Our books are available from your local or online booksellers or from Newmarket Press, 18 East 48th Street, New York, NY 10017; phone 212-832-3575 ext. 19 or 800-669-3903; fax 212-832-3629; email sales@newmarketpress.com. Price and availability are subject to change. Catalogs and information on quantity order discounts are available upon request.

www.newmarketpress.com